Carleton Beals

WAR
within a
WAR

The Confederacy Against
Itself

Chilton Books

A Division of Chilton Company
Publishers
Philadelphia and New York

Foreword

A century ago my grandfather, a devout Moravian, led a Union company of Ohio Volunteers through the red hills of Dade County in northern Alabama and on to Montgomery, once the proud capital of the Confederacy. Vaguely, though I was a tiny tot, I remember his telling years later how much he liked the people, how cordial and enthusiastic they were to him and his men. But, after all, he was in the heart of the region of the "war within a war."

Some years ago I crisscrossed his trail when I went to Scottsboro on a newspaper assignment. For a while I lived in the sharecropper shacks east of Montgomery, shivering in the 4-degree weather as the snow drifted in through the holes in the flimsy walls. I listened to an old-timer, his gnarled hands gripping his knotted cane, bemoaning the fact that he could not pay his two-year-old debt. It was seven cents! Fifteen years later I found many of those ragged, half-starved people cured of their pelagra and wearing decent clothes: even Negro girls had nice warm coats. They were working in the new defense industries. Cotton growers wailed over the scarcity of hands and had to offer unheard-of wages or let their crops molder in the fields. A boardinghouse keeper in a town farther south had grown sour over having to do her own cleaning and washing, with no servants available.

On my earlier trip I looked for free minds and souls in Montgomery and Birmingham and, of course, found many, though most of them were too frightened to talk. In Tuscaloosa I ate splendid wild strawberries and talked with university professors

3099

who had few restraints on their tongues, except for the gentility natural to their profession, and I marveled at the sudden desperate violence that had exploded beside traditional white columns and honeysuckled walls, and among the red trumpet vines hiding poverty-holed roofs. In Civil War days and thereafter violence had been more dreadful.

In Mobile, the Black Warrior town that had once heard the clank of De Soto's armor, I could find only Bible stores, but finally unearthed a small lavender-backed volume called *Mobile: Fact and Tradition*, the first book I had been able to find for sale about this magical state where the stars once fell, and where, according to author Clarence Cason, a loyal Southerner, the people live between antiquity and immaturity, yet have little interest in their antiquity—except that they live it and often enjoy it. Cason's fine little book is already thirty years old.

At one time or another, I have visited nearly all the places mentioned in *War Within a War*, including the rather dreary county seat of Winn Parish in Louisiana. The sturdy persistence of an abiding way of life reinforced my story.

This book makes no attempt to penetrate into the deeper mysteries of men and society in the South, but is merely an account of one facet of that colossal happening a hundred years ago, one aspect of the courage and abiding independence of thousands upon thousands of people caught in the soul-wrenching toils of the Civil War. They and their land were ruled by the slavocracy and led into darkness and defeat. Here is a glimpse of the struggle of the people who resisted the efforts of the men who seized power in 1861. Many paid for their convictions with their lives.

In numerous parts of the South, as in Natchez, Mississippi, in 1861, people, perhaps chiefly out of habit, celebrated Washington's birthday as usual. February 22 was exactly two weeks after the formation of the Confederacy at Montgomery by the representatives of the Secessionists in the first seven states that had left the Union. Some of the people celebrated because they considered the South to be more faithful to the doctrines of the American Revolution than was the North. But others did so because they were still ardently for the federal union in their minds and hearts and did not want secession or war, did not believe in slavery or fighting for it. Their reasons were many.

Over 80 per cent of the Southerners owned no slaves, though a large minority in one way or another were accustomed to the "peculiar institution," and were dependent upon it directly or indirectly for their livelihood or personal security. To oppose it in any way often brought fearful reprisals, not merely from the rich and powerful, but from neighbors. William H. Skaggs of Alabama wrote in his book, *The Southern Oligarchy*, "The great mass of the Southern people had no interest in slavery and they were bitterly opposed to it." The pro-Whig *Courier* of Natchez remarked, a week before the Washington's birthday celebration, "We live under an Oligarchy that has not yet dared to trust the people."

This book is about those people who resisted, because of their love for the Union, or civil rights, or because they believed the struggle to be a "rich man's war, poor man's fight." It is about those who hated conscription and its unfair exemptions for the favored few, those who fought the property seizures, who were dismayed at the looting and corruption before the war, during the war, and after, who were angry because their cotton was burned, and those who merely wanted to be left alone on their eroded little farms, in their creaking shacks and plow the red earth in the spring. For some, particularly the mountain people, similar resistance had gone on for a hundred years, often with armed violence, against the political monopoly and injustice of the plantation owners.

The edges of history grow blurred with time. As with the individual, the sorrows of society must be smoothed away, the sharper edges made dull, the tarnished blade brighter with romance. Little by little the Southern leaders have been reassimilated, by automatic or ingenious myth-making, as national heroes, which, whatever their notable qualities, they never were. It is natural, too, to stress the dramatic episodes of war, the dashing cavalry raids, the heroes of battle, the courage of individual soldiers and officers, and to forget the evil for which they were also fighting. The stories of those who refused to conform to the patriotic slogans of the Confederacy and suffered their own Golgotha, who resisted a vigilante terrorism rarely paralleled in history, have largely been lost. A veil was drawn over them at the time by the contemporary Civil War mythology and suppression; the veil has rarely been lifted. Here I have tried to look behind the curtain.

The significance of the war within a war was also hidden by the Northern victory, when those in the South who had fought for the Union were cast into the same slough of general disaster as the Secessionists and had to struggle for survival. Reconstruction tried to do many fine things for the stricken land, not always wisely or with proper knowledge, but the effort was largely destroyed by the carpetbaggers and scalawags seeking self-enrichment, by the Ku Klux Klan and the Knights of the White Camelia, and the restoration of the oligarchy to power—this time with the help of more selfish Northern interests. A new Southern mystique was created.

But this seemed to me an added reason for writing about the war within a war, about the people themselves rather than the glories of the war itself. I have tried to make this slight contribution to the actual history of the South, for it is not wise for the South or the country to forget the brave men who struggled for their rights and opinions even in wartime. The war within a war was well worth winning, and in the new forms it has taken in our own day is still worth winning. Many quiet but determined Southerners are engaged in that effort. Now and then quite a few are not so quiet.

This is not meant to be a book of opinion or controversy. It is written with love and admiration for brave, forgotten people of the South, and not for those who strutted in the limelight of power and authority for their brief day and hour (also brave men, convinced of the righteousness of their cause). That the system of slavery was a serious lapse in the history of Western civilization, that the Secessionists were trying to save a system already in decline, which was already disintegrating, need not overly concern us here. But what is often forgotten is that, as they progressively lost touch with their own people, they increasingly had to fight a war on two fronts, not merely at Vicksburg and Gettysburg, but behind the lines and in almost every town and village. It is possible to believe that the war against the North came alive, not so much out of fear of Northern abolitionists, but because of the crumbling society of the South itself. The men who ran the Confederacy would have had to face that inner war even had they not thrown the whole region into armed conflict with an outside enemy. It is, perhaps, one of the tragedies of history that Northern conquest halted, or at least distorted, an inevitable social process.

This book does not attempt to pose any such hypothetical historical possibilities. I have been interested only in showing how that war within a war developed, something of its growth and efforts, in the hope that this aspect of the great struggle may have significance both for the people of the South and for the country as a whole. In spite of the numerous ignoble elements involved, it is a story of those who believed that man, within the framework of his brief life span and the obstacles of nature and of history, is the maker of his own destiny and cannot escape his moral responsibilities. For these, among other reasons, I wrote this book.

CARLETON BEALS

Killingworth, Connecticut

Contents

WAR
within a
WAR

1. Solid South

At 6:30 A.M. the perfect spring day of April 12, 1861, a howitzer shell, fired from James Island near Charleston, South Carolina, arched toward brick-walled Fort Sumter on its tiny harbor island. At the uppermost curve, the white smoke accompanying its flight floated off into the higher air of heaven like a departing angel of peace. The Civil War had become an armed reality.

The phrase "solid South" seemed valid. Of about 2,000,000 white adults, 600,000 volunteered. There was tremendous enthusiasm and boastful confidence. Young recruits were sent off with great ovations, barbecues, balls, parades, and grandiloquent orations about the South's superiority, its valor, military skill, and chivalrous spirit. The South, men said, had donned her holiday attire; and wine cup, dance, and song ruled the hour.

The brave flags waved, and the romantic war mystique, which ruled the minds and hearts of so many Southerners, and in memory still does, strutted the stage for its little hour and day. But it was far from reflecting the thought and sentiments of the entire South. Even in that brief period of euphoria, the Confederacy was a divided land, a sick society, one already doomed to disaster. The cracks had been plastered over by a combination of demagoguery, political intrigue, delusion, and terrorism, but they soon widened and kept on widening until the whole edifice collapsed. The South's will to fight ebbed away faster than its crumbling supply lines.

For decades there had been revolt against economic and political control by the slaveowners, especially in the major cotton-growing states. Most Southerners owned no slaves, and the slave-owners were alarmed by the likelihood that suffrage would be widened to include the entire white population, even though literacy and property restrictions and gerrymandering continued to give them disproportionately large representation. Negroes, who could not vote, were counted in determining the number of representatives so counties containing few whites often had a larger number of legislators than those with few slaves.

Political privileges were reinforced by economic privileges. Though the slaves represented the largest part of the wealth in the South, the owner was taxed lightly, whereas the wage-earner and his meager property bore heavy burdens. The limited number of new industries suffered from similar feudal restrictions and heavy taxation. Little money was spent for improvements, but the few roads, railroads, canals, public buildings were constructed chiefly in the slave areas while other portions of the states re-

THE CONFEDERACY

The Confederacy. Areas of armed resistance before the end of 1863.

mained neglected. The slaveowners, observing that these injustices were being whittled down, that their controls were threatened, that revolt, or at least a more democratic order, was in the offing, were as much alarmed by such manifestations as by the handful of noisy abolitionists in the North. More than any threat of Northern coercion, secession and war arose from the fear of progress and freedom in the South itself.

Prior to the war there had been considerable free dialogue among whites. The secession issue had been hotly debated for decades. It had first flared up in the early 'thirties, with the South Carolina Nullification Acts, which had required the sending of Federal troops. Thereafter, more and more firebrands, rabid echoes of Calhoun's three decades of states' rights crusading, found secession and hate slogans profitable for political advancement, until finally they were able to shout down people of reason. But before freedom of speech was curtailed, more rational political debate remained active.

The dominant Democratic Party was long divided on the secession issue. In numerous states, such as Georgia, pro-Unionist elements defied the party bosses, set themselves up as independent parties, and won elections. The Whig Party, the wealthier and more conservative element, much of it slaveholding, had declined prior to the war, but was almost solidly pro-Union. The new Know-Nothing Party, anti-secession and antiwar, had come close to sweeping the whole South, had elected legislators, Congressmen, and Senators, and controlled major cities, such as Richmond, Alexandria, Atlanta, Raleigh, Mobile, Louisville, St. Louis, New Orleans, Galveston, and Austin. From Mississippi and Georgia to Tennessee, Union and Constitutional Union parties appeared. Many strong anti-Secessionists, such as Parson Brownlow of Tennessee and editor W. W. Holden of North Carolina, were pro-slavery but passionately devoted to the national government.

The so-called state conventions called on the eve of the war to consider secession still had strong pro-Unionist factions, but they were mostly rigged. The elections for the delegates were marked by terrorism, which in certain whole counties kept all but Secessionists from the polls. Often, out-of-state militiamen were rushed in to vote. Even so, all the conventions had strong anti-secession minorities, and some had anti-Secession majorities. In Virginia and Arkansas they were overwhelming. Texas and, for a time, Tennessee and North Carolina refused to call any conventions. In Texas the prowar people set up their own convention to railroad the state into war. Throughout all the states, pro-Union delegates were threatened, terrorized, and even in a few instances manhandled, to coerce them into changing their positions. Then with the seizure of Fort Sumter, the tide of prowar feeling suddenly flared so dangerously that Virginia, North Carolina, and Tennessee were stampeded into joining the parade of seceding states.

But large areas—east Tennessee, western and southwestern Virginia, western North Carolina, northern Alabama and Mississippi, and whole counties in Georgia, Louisiana, and Texas—remained hostile to the new Confederacy and opposed it, many times with weapons in hand. Before long, armed bands of pro-Unionists, draft-dodgers, and deserters roamed about in every state (including South Carolina), disrupting society, breaking down authority, forcing the recall of troops from the front, and weakening the whole war effort. Some marched across Virginia, Alabama, and Mississippi, waving the Stars and Stripes. Some counties, as in Georgia, long refused to lower the United States flag.

Reasons for this resistance, besides loyalty to the Federal Union, included opposition to slavery, resentment of the privileges of the well-to-do, particularly slaveowners (which generated the slogan, "rich man's war, poor man's fight"), resentment of favoritism to the wealthy in draft exemptions, plus discomfort from the growing hardships and dislocations due to the war itself—the scarcity of food, the terrible inflation and the impressment laws allowing army seizure of property, including both slaves and food.

The situation of white workers and artisans had become difficult in a slave society of low standards. More and more plantation owners were hiring out their skilled black workers as carpenters, masons, and the like, which further injured white workers.

Quick disillusionment came when Richmond boasts that Washington would be occupied within three months proved to be a cruel hoax.

The Quakers occupied several western counties in North Carolina and were strong in Texas, and elsewhere, the Germans, Irish, and other latter-day immigrants were pacifists against any and all war. So were many old-time Virginians and most mountaineers. The Quakers were also against slavery. Many had freed their own slaves and had paid to ship some back to Africa or to Northern asylum. Prior to the rise of cotton as the dominant product, there were probably more antislavery societies in the South than in the North, and many such groups persisted right up to the war and beyond.

Though the majority of the slaves remained loyal to their masters during the war, after the Emancipation Proclamation great numbers became disaffected, and thousands ran off, or began dragging their feet in the fields, thus reducing food production and causing difficulties of all sorts. Freedom was at hand and, before the end, sections of the South were threatened with slave uprisings that alarmed even Northern commanders. From the start, fear of a Negro revolt caused states to withhold soldiers from the front, even more so when these fears bloomed into actual possibilities. When the South finally realized it had to use black soldiers, prominent Southerners, even General Lee, began saying the South would have to emancipate all slaves. (Lee had freed his long before.) The shakiness of the Confederacy was apparent even to die-hard slaveowners. Though President Davis made special speaking trips to stem the growing antislavery agitation, which he equated with subversion against the Confederacy, the later Negro draft law itself cut away the very heart of the war, for it announced to all the world that the purpose of the war for slavery had never been justified, that four years of bloody death had been a futile, almost ridiculous, sacrifice.

As was said earlier, much of the flag-waving enthusiasm of the first days had been falsely generated, a delusion of wartime hysteria, created by demagogues and well-directed propaganda. Presbyterian minister John H. Aughey of Mississippi quoted many of these speakers: In battle one Southerner was the equivalent of ten Northern hirelings; the Northerners were riffraff mongrels, the scum of Europe, the mudsills of Yankeedom; the Yankees were flat-headed, nigger-stealing fanatics, inferior and cowardly; Lincoln was a baboon, an abominable white-livered abolitionist; Southerners were cavaliers, gentlemen who knew the grace of living; they were patricians. Such rantings aroused self-adulation, hot passions, and brutality, and impelled the long-suffering sharecroppers and the white dwellers in shacks to terrorize and silence everyone who was suspected of being opposed to slavery or in favor of the Union.

It was amazing how many of this ilk believed *themselves* to be highborn patricians, and were thus influenced to rush to enlist. Above all, those from the eastern seaboard really believed this myth of personal superiority, for they had long considered everybody above the fall line, the inland folk, to be barbarous and backward. "There just ain't no gentlemen up there," remarked a ragged white crab-hunter of the coast marshes to Upper Falls fishermen he was guiding.

Of course many volunteers came from the flower of the South. The members of the famous South Carolina Hampton outfit went forth to battle in carriages with trunks of fine clothes and personal belongings, and at least one black body-servant each. Their uniforms were dazzling. It was thus they rode into Richmond to twirl their mustachios at the fair ladies. In due time survivors would return by that same road, barefoot through snow and slush, ragged, wounded, mutilated, sick unto death, to join the ranks of the poor they had long despised.

The majority of volunteers, however, were poverty-stricken. How could it be otherwise? Most of these, as conservative William Watts Ball of South Carolina and Parson Brownlow of Tennessee noted, were better clothed and ate better food than they had ever known. Some, when asked why they were fighting, replied: "So we can take slaves into the territories," though their own families had never owned a slave. Others believed the Confederate government's promise, never kept, that it would take care of their families while they were off fighting.

Many writers have presented the war as a broader struggle to preserve something known as Southern culture and sovereignty. But regardless of such smoke screen arguments as "states' rights" and "maintaining the constitution," Vice President Alexander Stephens, in his famous early speech at Savannah, made it clear, as had the South Carolina Articles of Secession, that the key to the struggle was slavery and white supremacy: "With us, all the white race, however high or low, rich or poor, is equal in the eyes of the law. Not so with the Negro. Subordination is his place. He by Nature, or by the curse against Cain, is fitted for that condition which he occupies in our system." Experience, he continued, had taught Southerners that such subordination was best not only for the superior but the inferior race. Furthermore, it conformed to the ordinance of the Creator. Thus, nudging God, basing his argument on a biblical curse, he declared that slavery was the cornerstone of that new edifice, the Confederacy. Ironically he soon abandoned Richmond to become an opponent of practically all wartime measures and one of its most persistent peace advocates long before peace actually came.

Well before Fort Sumter, a reign of terror, even though resisted in numerous areas, brutally silenced most of those opposed to slavery or secession. This violence, often abetted by wealthy plantation holders and slaveowners, was carried on chiefly by the lowest, poorest, and most illiterate elements, long frustrated, among whom submerged hate now erupted to the surface as ugly aggression. Such creatures were often egged on by that scarcely credible animal, the rural Southern preacher, though many less bigoted men of the cloth were themselves beaten, jailed, and driven out. The riffraff was egged on by political demagogues and by officeholders threatened with exposure for corruption and theft. It was an opportunity for nasty little men, long ground under, to give vent to their grudges, get even with neighbors by burning their property, stealing their livestock, even hanging or shooting those suspected of antiwar sentiments. Whole families were jailed or driven to the highways. Any pretext served; anybody believed to have said anything against slavery—even years back—or who had taken a stand against secession, or supported a Unionist candidate for the state conventions, anybody who doubted the success or wisdom of the Confederate effort, was in danger of death.

With war, in many places the bench was deserted by judges, and the local courts ceased to exist or were seized by shysters (the Federal courts were out of business entirely), so prior criminal accusations and civil actions lapsed, and accused prisoners were freed. Vigilantes held their own courts in barns, woods, and creek bottoms and imposed their own death sentences, or killed without any formalities whatever.

Such terrorism was already rampant by the time elections were held for the prowar conventions. The Reverend John H. Aughey of Mississippi, in strongly pro-Unionist north-central Choctaw County, listened to a Secessionist candidate shout, "We have glorious news from Tallahatchee County [also pro-Unionist]. Seven Tory [1] submissionists were hanged there in one day, and the so-called Unionist candidates, having the wholesome dread of hemp before their eyes, are not canvassing the county; therefore the heretical doctrine of submission . . . disgraces not their county." Reason and fair play had flown the coop. By such terrorism most of the Secessionist conventions were chosen, and state after state was taken out of the Union.

At the polls, Aughey asked for a Union ballot. None had been printed, and he was told menacingly he'd better vote for the Secessionist ticket. Instead he wrote out and deposited a Union ballot amid frowns, murmurs, and threats from the judges and bystanders. His was the only pro-Union vote cast.

His book *Tupelo* (the name of a state prison), written long after his own escape from his persecutors, is full of accounts of

---

[1] This strange rendering was in common use.

how vigilantes and soldiers, often drunk, tortured and murdered victims, many of them educated men of high standing. His stories could be duplicated all over the South.

As soon as war began, an old Negro slave brought him an order to appear before a vigilante tribunal. The paper was crudely illustrated with skull and crossbones, a newly made grave, and an old man with his hands bound behind his back, a cap over his face, standing upon the trap of a gallows, labeled, "Such is the doom of all traitors."

> Parson John H. Aughey, your treasonable proclivities are known. You have been reported to us as one of the disaffected whose presence is a standing menace to the perpetuity and prosperity of our newly organized government—the Confederate States of America. Your name heads the proscribed list. You are ordered to appear on tomorrow afternoon at two o'clock before our Vigilante Committee in W. H. Simpson's carriage shop to answer to the charges of treason and abolitionism.
>
> By order of the Vigilantes
> K. K. K. and K. G. C.

Aughey boldly presented himself. The chief spokesman of the dozen persons present was a Methodist preacher, John Locke Armstrong, recently expelled by his own congregation. He was a great Nimrod who boasted that in five months he had killed 48 racoons, 200 squirrels, 10 deer and had captured 10 runaway slaves with bloodhounds. One judge was the ruling elder in Aughey's own church; another was a one-eyed, hard-shell Baptist. There were various "Rock Angels," so-called because they lived in caves. Only three or four knew how to read or write. A mysterious Major John Mecklin was present.

Reverend Locke began. "Parson Aughey, you have been reported to us as holding abolition sentiments, and as being disloyal to the Confederate States."

"*Who reported me, and where are your witnesses?*"

"Anyone has a right to report, and it is optional whether he confronts the accused or not. . . ."

"*Proceed then with the trial in your own way.*"

". . . Did you ever say that you did not believe that God ordained the institution of slavery?"

"*I believe that God did not ordain the institution of slavery.*"

"Did not God command the Israelites to buy slaves from the Canaanite nations? . . ."

"*The Canaanites had filled their cup of iniquity to overflowing, and God* [the Hebrew nationalist war god] *commanded the Israelites to exterminate them; this . . . they failed to do. God afterwards permitted the Hebrews to reduce them to . . . servitude; but the punishment . . . does not justify war or the slave trade.*"

"Did you say that you were opposed to slavery which existed in the house of Christ?"

"*I did, because the system . . . was cruel in the extreme. You yourself profess to be opposed to white slavery. . . .*"

"Did you tell Mr. Creath that you knew some Negroes who were better in every respect than some white men?"

"*I said that I knew some Negroes who were better classical scholars than any white man I had yet met in Choctaw County . . . Some . . . were prominent for virtue and holiness.*"

After a lot of such long-winded nonsense, Locke called for a vote on the fate of the accused.

"Put me down in favor of hanging," said fat Simon Bolivar, one of the Rock Angels. "Better men nor him hez been hung in the county lately, an' it has done good. I cain't see no reason why he shouldn't hang."

A big crowd gathered outside, and the mysterious Mecklin said sardonically that the court had better adjourn at once, that many people thought the court illegal, and its members might have to answer for the proceedings. Locke, an arrant coward, turned pale, ducked out back, and got away through the woods.

Aughey's friends provided him with arms. In the night the vigilantes surrounded his house. He cocked both barrels of his shotgun and sat facing the door, determined to shoot the first man who broke in. Several ran to the woodshed to get a battering ram but butted into a wire clothesline. One was knocked unconscious, and several, badly injured, howled like beaten hounds. Two volleys of gunfire were heard and all the would-be assassins fled. Two fell into the well, and one died of his injuries.

Aughey's friends appeared. He wrote, "We named this the Battle of Wyandotte, the name of my home. Probably the first blood of the war was shed in this encounter."

But he was thrown out of his pulpit; another man, mistaken for him, was killed, and he and his wife and daughter had to flee for their lives, closely pursued by mobsters. Presently he was arrested, held in fetters in Tupelo prison in Lee County, and condemned to death.

Typical was the experience of Herman Bledsoe, a pro-Unionist in East Tennessee. A giant, six feet and eight inches tall, he was taken from his home along with his wife and two children. The vigilantes condemned him to be burned alive, just as, the previous week, a Colonel Browne's slave, Sam, had been burned alive. He was tied to a sapling and faggots were heaped about him, but one of the ringleaders, bringing the wood, slipped a knife to him, then harangued the mob with patriotic speech.

Bledsoe cut himself free. "Looking back from a hill about two miles distant," he related, "I saw the flames rising higher and higher . . . suddenly I heard howls of disappointment and rage."

An old Negro slave and his wife nursed him back to health, and he set out with twenty-five others to escape to the Federal lines. A posse caught up with them. Fifty Confederates were killed, and also most of those trying to escape. Bledsoe and a few survivors fled on, wounded and bleeding.

The terror mounted on all sides, for, in spite of the response to the drums of war, hundreds of thousands of citizens were apathetic or bitterly opposed; many tried in every way to aid the Union. From the outset whole counties and whole regions refused to fight, and some areas organized at once to protect themselves against terrorism. Soon in every state, armed bands of Unionists, deserters, conscripts, and others fought off the civil and military authorities. Groups numbering hundreds, sometimes thousands, hid in the hills or roamed about lawlessly, often looting, burning, and killing. A year after the war began, many of these came openly, and armed, to the polling places, and in Tennessee, Alabama, Mississippi, North Carolina, and Georgia, numerous pacifists or Union sympathizers were sent to the State legislature or to Congress. In Texas, Sam Houston, thrown out of the governorship because he opposed secession, and who continued thereafter to call the Confederate President "Little Dictator Jeffie Davis," by 1863 was asked to run again for the office, but declined.

The first really big tempest in all Southern states arose over President Davis' Conscription Act, which called on every man from 18 to 30 to register. Later the age limits were extended to include almost all adult males. The draft act coincided with the expiration of short-term enlistments, and morale plummeted when men found they were to be held in the army for the duration. Many deserted. Even loyal Southerners considered the law bungling and unfair. The provision that angered most, as in the North, was that permitting a draftee to buy a substitute. Also those owning or overseeing slaves were allowed an exemption for each twenty (later fifteen) Negroes, enough to keep plantation owners and all their male relatives who were cowards out of the fighting. Senator James Phelan of Mississippi wrote Davis that the law had met with universal odium, chiefly because of slave-owner exemptions. Draft boards, as in all wars, favored rich evaders and gave exemptions to important and influential people. The slogan "a rich man's war, poor man's fight" began to echo on all sides.

Opposition was also fanned by military abuses, as noted in Georgia L. Tatum's fine work, *Disloyalty in the Confederacy*. One conscript dropped off at his home to see his dying wife. When he asked leave to bury her, he was shot as a deserter. A West Pointer, General Braxton Bragg, among other strict officers, shot men for petty misdemeanors or mistakes, and desertions increased.

Everywhere conscription was opposed, obstructed, or flouted by the people and many local officials, even by state executives, particularly in Georgia and North Carolina. All the governors objected to parts of the law. They were particularly vehement over favoritism toward the influential and wealthy. Most were outraged by the out-of-state conscription officers, who strutted about in fancy uniforms, and appeared in carriages with numerous black servants. The War Department was repeatedly warned that conscripts would refuse to answer the call.

More and more the epithet "dictator" was hurled at Davis. W. W. Holden of Raleigh, editor of North Carolina's leading daily, the *Eastern Standard*, wrote in mid-1863 concerning conscription and other abuses: "We know now that no people ever lost their liberties at once, but step by step, as some deadly disease steals upon the system and gradually but surely saps the fountain of life. . . . The argument now is, we hate Lincoln so bitterly that in order to resist him successfully we must make slaves of ourselves." If Davis assumed dictatorial powers, North Carolina would necessarily withdraw from the Confederacy, he said.

Out of fear of dictatorship, of slave revolts, of armed deserters, partly to insure a proper work force, and, shortly, because of the growing cries for peace, various governors, particularly Joseph Brown of Georgia, often refused to let new conscripts leave the state, demanded the return of the twelve-month volunteers, and even tried to call back militia units.

The subsequent Impressment Laws were even more unpopular and aroused much opposition, this time from the powerful as well as the poor. These acts permitted the army to take slaves, wagons, livestock, food, and provisions at prices arbitrarily set, but always below the market rate. Even the South Carolina legislators, along with those of other states, passed resolutions against such seizures. Florida's governor, John Milton, accused army agents of seizing all the produce, even from women and children, whose small plots at best never produced sufficient food, leaving them, as well as those better off, to starve. He declared it to be his duty to protect rights, lives, and liberty against such agents. Governor Brown protested bitterly against the seizure of all supplies from certain communities, leaving them starving, while nothing was taken from other neighborhoods. He called it stealing and robbing by unauthorized individuals, and predicted—and this was borne out—that the alienated farmers in future would plant only what was necessary for their own families.

Georgia plantation owner, and Davis' first Secretary of State, Robert Toombs, a vocal apostle of Jeffersonian ideas, told the Georgia legislature that capitalists, merchants, manufacturers, and speculators had been allowed to remain home and amass fortunes without being taxed, while farmers and agriculturists were being stripped; they were the real sufferers, both in blood and treasure. As a result not one acre in fifty of the best corn land of Georgia was being planted. He himself defied the farm restrictions, vowing he would plant whatever acreage and crops he wished. Robert Taliaferro Hunter of Virginia, Davis' second Secretary of State, who also left the cabinet in a huff, took the same recalcitrant position. Thus both the poor farmers and sharecroppers, reduced to near starvation, and the wealthy plantation owners, deprived of the right to profit and to profiteer, clamored against property impressment.

Resentment was not allayed by the fact that agents and officers carrying out impressment were usually from out of state—mostly Marylanders and Virginians, Holden noted. Both Brown of Georgia and Vance of North Carolina were bitter about this; their sentiments were echoed by Milton of Florida and by others elsewhere.

The Tax-in-Kind Law (1863) which took one-tenth of all farm production for the government, was equally resented, especially as neither land nor slaves were properly taxed—further evidence of "rich man's war, poor man's fight." "It's them rich fellers who are making this war," said an old Georgia farmer, "and keeping their precious bodies out of harm's way. They've all run off, one so fast that dominoes could've been played on his shirttail. My own poor brother is lying ill with smallpox in Macon, working for eleven dollars a month and now for a year not getting a penny, only eleven thousand bullets a minute." Governor Zebulon Vance of North Carolina accused the Richmond government of taking fighting men with one hand and a tenth of their substance with the other. To add to difficulties, the 1862 crops were poor.

King Cotton, God Cotton, proved to have clay feet that began to crumble soon after war began. Cotton, it had been argued, would bring victory to the South, force the closing down of Northern mills and bring France and England hurrying to aid. It did not work out that way. As the blockade cut into the exports of cotton, its price rose 1000 per cent on the European market, but dropped to nearly nothing in the South, where cotton piled up in warehouses often had to be burned to be kept out of Federal hands—an act of destruction which most planters blamed on Davis, not the Yankees, with whom they could have made good deals. The high European price brought little benefit for the Confederate government, little to the growers. It benefited only blockade runners and speculators. The growers angrily blamed the government for bungling the whole matter. Hopeful that their own cotton would be smuggled out, they grew twice as angry at curtailment of cotton acreage to force the growing of foodstuffs.

But if the price of cotton went down, the prices of everything else went up. As more and more currency and treasury notes flooded the country, speculators hoarded all goods in short supply. Coffee, tea, and other urgently needed imports became almost unobtainable; prices for both luxuries and necessities skyrocketed. People took their money home in a basket and brought back their purchases in their purses. As early as 1862, inflation made it almost impossible to buy food, and people around Natchez called for martial law to deal with speculators. Even the hoarders and smugglers became angry over the soaring prices of the kinds of merchandise they did not control.

In January of that year, the Clarksville *Chronicle* of middle Tennessee complained:

When we think of the self-sacrificing patriotism of our brave volunteers, and then look at the shylocks at home who extort the last cent from their families for the necessities of life, the contrast is painfully disgusting. . . . The country will learn, to its cost, that men will not volunteer to fight its battles, leaving their dependent wives and daughters to the tender charities of the sharpers . . . who speculate upon the scanty pittance of daily bread. . . . The time is not far distant when Judge Lynch will pass sentence upon such merciless and heartless speculators.

The high prices for drygoods, clothing, and food, the *Eastern Clarion* said, were reducing a large share of the population to pauperdom. Some belated legal protection was provided for destitute families of volunteers, but as inflation got worse, hunger and injustices became greater. Opposition grew on every side.

After the fall of Vicksburg, Mississippi and Alabama were swept clean of supplies by scores of Federal raids. The cutting off of the West meant that much of the South had little chance any longer of getting enough food. Before the end, even well-to-do people were reduced to living on bread and water for months at a time. Money became almost worthless. Few had any, for banks closed down and wages ceased. Millions came near starving. Nearly everybody, except patriotic war profiteers, senior politicians, and high officers, had to tighten his belt. Davis' own large salary could not provide enough for his family and toward the end, the state banks would not honor his personal check for some $28,000.

As Grant clearly saw, with the fall of Vicksburg in 1863 and the loss of the Mississippi River, the fate of the Confederacy was sealed. Increasingly serious food riots were sparked by hungry civilians and even soldiers. Twice Galveston was menaced with looting and violence. In nearly every town and city, such riots sometimes became actions bordering on open insurrection. In Richmond itself one riot could not be quelled by police or militia. Single-handed and bravely, President Davis finally quieted it with eloquent unfulfillable promises.

A North Carolina woman, Mrs. Cornelius Phillips Spencer,

whom Governor Vance called the smartest woman in the state, wrote vividly of the hysteria, fear, indignation, sorrow, and final despair. Though a few rich planters banqueted until the end, families of the highest respectability and refinement had to live on cornbread, sorghum, and peas, rarely a bit of meat, never any tea or coffee. Dried apples and peaches were a luxury. Children had to go barefoot through the winter. Every day panic-stricken refugees brought fresh tales of horror and ruin.

As armies seesawed across state after state, communities were further disrupted by hordes of refugees—men, women, children —fleeing before the path of galloping hooves and flaming guns. Those who remained in the track of war were robbed, their homes and barns looted or burned. They were killed if they resisted, and often were killed anyway. Negro refugees, though many squatted in or near Federal lines, where they usually could get food, had a particularly dreadful time. Northern soldiers were encouraged to live off the countryside, something Confederate troops were forbidden to do except when on Northern soil. As the roving bands of draft-resisters and deserters grew and spread, still more property was pillaged.

Davis denounced the clamor for states' rights—against the Confederacy this time—and the open advocacy of the abolition of slavery in every state, both of which he called treason. He had Congress suspend *habeas corpus*. This aroused such fury and was so openly flouted by some governors, that it had to be abandoned. But on June 2, 1864, Davis again called for suspension in order better to handle critics and deserters who roamed in great bands in every state. One immediate result was the temporary suspension of Holden's North Carolina *Standard*. But the law could not be enforced. Local authorities nearly everywhere disregarded it as did some of the state authorities. Prisoners, thus held without due process, were sometimes freed by arms. The military tried imposing martial law, but opposition was so strong that Richmond had to forbid its exercise by the generals unless specifically authorized.

Another bone of contention in seaboard and Gulf states was

the attempt to control the operations of blockade runners. Richmond's regulations commandeered shipping space so the central government could realize profits from the tenfold prices of cotton in Europe and to force the shipping in of war materials, instead of luxuries which were less bulky and more profitable to the private runners. Most officials evaded the new regulations. Brown openly defied them. Vance said bitterly in his 1864 message to the General Assembly that the arbitrary Confederate measures had forced him to withdraw North Carolina state-owned vessels from the trade. The *Ad-Vance,* on which he had relied to bring in absolute necessities, had been captured because the Confederate cruiser *Tallahassee* had seized her coal, forcing her to put to sea with inferior North Carolina coal. This, in turn, reduced her speed and made such a smudge she was easily followed and seized. Not all the armed cruisers together had been as important as the *Ad-Vance,* and their concentration in North Carolina ports, far from providing protection, had brought on such a swarm of Northern gunboats that blockade runners could no longer get through.

South Carolina, the leader of secession, where local patriotism had been fanned to fever heat in a pandemonium of hysterical joy when Fort Sumter was taken, soon became a divided state. Angered over conscription and other laws, the citizens grumbled and snarled. The legislature bitterly denounced the property impressment agents, who ignored the piled up 10 per cent in-kind supplies, and seized other goods right and left. But much of the stored tax produce was scattered in local barns and warehouses off the beaten track, and roads and railroads were falling into disrepair.

As early as the spring of 1862 the Fort Sumter garrison—in the very citadel of Secessionist glory—threatened mutiny and openly refused to fire on the enemy. An arrest was made, whereupon guns were spiked and five men deserted. The Charleston commander asked for fresh troops to reestablish Charleston's confidence in the garrison. But charges of disloyalty continued throughout the year and beyond, and the port inhabitants were repeatedly in panic. Soon enough, South Carolina, too, was harassed in all her mountain counties, and in others as well, by bands of malcontents and deserters. Robert Barnwell Rhett, editor of the *Mercury*, the greatest firebrand of the South, called for Davis' impeachment. Varina Davis confessed to friends she had come to hate him more than any Black Republican in Washington.

Nearly all Georgians believed in the right of secession though a large share of them had not wished to exercise it. A third of the state convention delegates, in spite of the way it had been rigged, had been opposed to it. The dissidents had been led by Alexander Stephens and Herschel V. Johnson. Stephens' brother and Johnson were the most powerful political bosses in the state, and Johnson had been Vice-Presidential candidate on the (Northern) Douglas Democratic ticket in the fateful 1860 national elections. Years before, he had broken the Know-Nothing conspiracy by campaigning with gun and whip in hand. Many of these dissidents and others soon came to advocate secession from the Confederacy, a step frequently suggested by the governor himself.

After war came, various Georgia mountain counties refused to lower the Stars and Stripes and kept on making trouble. When asked to cut down the courthouse flagpole in Jasper, in north central Pickens County, Governor Brown refused. "By no means. Let it float. It floated over our fathers and we all love the flag. . . . Let them do it. I will send no troops to interfere with it."

Even before the end of 1861, even many strong proslavery people turned against the Confederacy or became peace advocates. Georgia's best-known leaders increasingly criticized the Confederate Government. Such men as Brown, Vice-President Stephens, Toombs, Johnson, Joshua Hill were vociferous about Davis' encroachments on Georgia's rights. As ruin spread, they called ever more loudly for peace, declaring that the resources of the South were exhausted.

From 1863 on, peace meetings in Georgia and throughout the Confederacy were called openly. Grant detected a strong sentiment for peace, often strongly pro-Union around Vicksburg. Presently those in favor of peace advised General Sherman that his occupation of Georgia met with their approval and they would aid him in every way possible. Sherman promised all such protection against reprisals and offered arms for them to protect themselves. Form a league, he advised, and he would protect all members in their homes and get their produce to market. Governor Brown's actions at this time, such as disbanding the militia, obstructed resistance and, intentionally or otherwise, furthered Sherman's success.

The Governor of North Carolina, a breadstuff and tobacco area rather than a cotton state, had refused to call a special convention to consider secession until Lincoln's call for troops. Even then the vote in Raleigh was 9 to 1 pro-Union, in the state at large 2 to 1, but by the time the convention met, pressure was too great, and all voted to secede. The Secessionist delegates cheered and threw their hats into the air, but the Conservatives and Unionists sat dourly silent. It was like a sea partly in storm, but with a large part ominously calm. Thereafter, Unionist leaders became active, secretly obstructing the Confederacy and pushing agitation. Secret peace societies flourished more than elsewhere, though they came to honeycomb the entire South. Throughout the struggle, North Carolina was one of the most overtly antiwar states.[2]

W. W. Holden, editor of the *Standard*, soon advocated secession from the Confederacy! He had fought secession tooth and nail at the 1860 Charleston Democratic convention, where the party had split into three factions. He told the people that if the state had a right to secede from the United States, it now had the right to get out of the Confederacy—and with more reason. He ridiculed Governor Clark's slogan "to the last man and the last dollar," and denounced the harsh political monopoly by the Secessionists and Democrats. He promoted peace meetings and reported them at length in his paper. In the August, 1862, elections he called for the election of men in favor of peace, including the "Federal" candidate, Zebulon B. Vance, a prominent

---

[2] Yet its troops were among the finest in the Confederate army.

Whig. Vance received a 2 to 1 vote even among the war volunteers, while in Quaker counties, such as Guildford, Randolph, and Forsyth, his vote was 19 to 1. The new state assembly had a big propeace majority.

At once Vance and state officials began releasing men who were against the war and also deserters and protecting them. The Assembly forced the Confederate authorities to release a preacher who had been accused of spying and taken off to Richmond. Despite the law, *habeas corpus* was granted by nearly all the courts.

Holden was behind much of it. He used the hated draft law as a whip to arouse the people, particularly the poor and non-slaveowners. The war, he insisted, should be a voluntary one! Conscription wiped out every vestige of constitutional liberty. He demanded that special privileges be taken away from the plantation owners, that they be taxed for their slaves, so that independent farmers, tradespeople, and the poor did not bear most of the burden.

In the 1863 elections, he wrote that the demand for an honorable peace flashed like fire throughout the state. Within eight weeks, one hundred peace meetings were held. But the Confederacy and North Carolina, remarked Major John W. Moore in his *School History of North Carolina* (p. 280), merely waded deeper into the crimson flood, though eight of the ten North Carolinians sent to the Confederate Congress were out-and-out peace men, and Vance warned Davis that peace sentiment was so strong that it could be assuaged and order restored only by starting peace negotiations with the North.

For years Holden cried, "Peace! Peace! Peace! North Carolina has done enough. Do no more. The constitution as it was! The Union as it was!" General D. H. Hill, the local commander, wanted to arrest him but dared not do so.

However, on the night of September 9, 1863, a Georgia regiment en route to the front sacked the *Standard* office and tossed the type into the street. Holden had to take refuge in the governor's mansion. The next day he rang the bells of the city to call out armed citizens who proceeded to sack and burn the rival newspaper. The attack on the *Standard* could not have occurred without upper-bracket instigation, and when a few days later another outrage by out-of-state troops occurred, Vance asked Davis to send no more troops through Raleigh or he would re-call the North Carolina troops from the field so they could de-fend their homes.

A few days before the final debacle, Holden wrote: "Up to the hour when the states south of us madly shot from their ap-propriate orbits in the federal system, the hands of the federal government had never been laid upon them but to protect and defend them. The old flag never waved whether on land or sea but for their protection. . . . Let us hope, that the same flag, restored to its original place in the heavens, will wave as our flag, once and forever."

President Johnson called him to Washington and appointed him provisional governor. One of his first proclamations guaranteed Negroes the full protection of the law in preserving their liberty, their property, and payment of their wages.

In the northern half of Alabama, a majority opposed secession, and every northern county sent pro-Union Cooperationists to the war convention, though they claimed it lacked sovereignty. The North Alabamans were Whigs or Unionists, and their chief, Wil-liam R. Smith, had been the Know-Nothing floor leader in Con-gress. Nicholas Davis of Madison County retorted to William Yancey's cry, "Traitors!" that the North Alabamans would meet the Secessionists at the foot of the mountains and decide the is-sue at the point of the bayonet.

The whole area became a major center for deserters from all Southern states, and the army was never able to round them up. Revolt spread into all corners of the state. In Jones County of the far South, an independent republic is said to have been set up.

In both Alabama and Mississippi, investigator Robert B. Blount said, the Unionists had instituted such a reign of terror that peo-ple were afraid of their shadows. In April, 1864, a clandestine Alabama convention held in the joining corners of Winston,

Fayette, and Marin counties, voted to remain neutral until Federal troops could arrive, but groups bearing the Stars and Stripes crossed into Mississippi to arouse Unionists there.

Early that winter, a General P. D. Roddy, with his brother-in-law, a major and other officers, negotiated directly for peace with the Federal authorities, saying that all counties north of the main cotton belt and even those in the southeast were anxious to return to the Union and that peace candidates would sweep the elections. The negotiators asked Washington to announce a plan for gradual emancipation with indemnification so as not to alarm slaveowners. If Governor T. H. Watts would not accept the terms offered, they would set up a new civilian-military government, and nearly all Alabama soldiers would support it. Whole counties seceded from the Confederacy and prepared to make a separate peace. The Governor himself hastened to advocate a separate peace. Before the scheme ripened, the Confederate forces were defeated everywhere.

That Kansas would remain in the Union was never in doubt. Well before the main curtain went up, a bloody civil war had been fought there between proslavery men, aided by massive expeditions from Missouri, and New England emigrés armed with Sharps rifles provided by Boston abolitionists. John Brown, his sons and followers, burned farms and freed slaves. President Buchanan, who favored the slavery elements, put a price of $3,000 on his head.

Reverend Martin White told the Kansas Lecompton proslavery legislature graphically and humorously how he had killed John Brown's son Frederick in the bloody Osawatomie fight. That same night the minister's body was found lying out on the prairie.

By and large the Free Soil Kansans had won out before the war began, and they provided veteran fighters of great valor for the Union Army. They were also incorrigible and remorseless thieves.

Neighboring Missouri was dominated largely by powerful Southern elements and kept in the Union, where her true interests lay, only by a hair's breadth. The rule of the great senator, Thomas H. Benton, was over. Many times he had warned his people of the slavery conspiracy to divide the Union, and by 1861 there was a big Free Soil movement, especially in St. Louis where there was a large German population led by Franz Siegel. But Governor Claiborne F. Jackson refused to accede to Lincoln's call for volunteers for the "nefarious purpose of subduing the South." Though unsuccessful in forcing secession, he set up pro-Confederate training centers. To counter this Captain Nathaniel Lyon, in charge of the United States arsenal in St. Louis, energetically organized volunteer pro-Union regiments, mostly German. They divided the state into rival armed camps. When the prewar seizure of the arsenal was threatened, Lyon put the arms on board a river boat and sent them to Alton, Illinois.

Shortly afterward 6,000 Federal soldiers forced the surrender of the Confederate camp with its 1,200 Southern militia, plus much ammunition and twenty cannon. In all, 100,000 Missourians joined the Federal armies while 30,000 joined Confederate forces.

The Arkansas convention in March, 1861, voted down the Secession Ordinance by a decisive majority. The northwest counties were overwhelmingly against leaving the Union. But fanatic proslavery elements began terrorizing these counties. The governor refused to send state forces to aid Lincoln, and on May 6 reassembled the convention. It was boycotted by the pro-Unionists. Hence it showed only one vote against secession. At once the frontiersmen, mountaineers, and Irish immigrants of the northwest organized for armed resistance. There was established the first secret, anti-Confederate, peace society. Certain pro-Union meetings were held openly.

In August 1862, the authorities arrested 200 members of an armed regiment of resisters. Before the end of the year, the death penalty was set up for anybody assisting the enemy. But desertions increased and soon the flow of recruits to the Union forces became a river. By December eight Arkansas regiments, black and white, had been built up as a Federal force. Southeastern Perry County, with only 600 volunteers, sent a company of 94 armed men to aid the Union Army. So little were Confederate recruits trusted that they were drilled at Fort Smith without arms.

Union General Samuel R. Curtis, military head of the Department of Missouri, warmly welcomed everywhere, reported that the people seemed ready to abandon the Confederacy, and General E. R. Brown reported that up to 5,000 men in West Arkansas could be quickly armed to fight the Confederacy, that refugees were coming in droves into all Federal posts. Confederate General E. W. Ganut frankly admitted that Arkansas' loyalty to Jefferson Davis did not extend beyond the shadow of his army, and that hatred of him and his cause was widespread and intense. He called attention to pro-Union meetings, desertions, oaths of allegiance to the United States and enlistments in the Northern army. People northwest of Little Rock were mocking openly at the Confederate conscription and impressment agents who appeared in carriages with large retinues of gallant gentlemen and Negro boys.

The increasing exactions by Confederate eastern agents, added to the failure of the Confederacy to provide the state with proper protection, soon outraged the most loyal. Governor Henry P. Rector said hotly, "It was for liberty, that Arkansas struck, and not for subordination. If arteries of the Confederate heart do not permeate beyond the eastern bank of the Mississippi, let southern Missourians, Arkansans, Texans, all the great West know it and prepare for the future. Arkansas lost, abandoned, subjugated—is not Arkansas a Confederate State?—desolated as a wilderness. Her children fleeing from the wrath to come, will build them a new ark and launch it on new waters, seeking an independent haven of equality and safety and rest." It was a feeble echo of Aaron Burr, who had schemed long ago to set up an independent country in the southwest, and it meant nothing in the long run.

When Sam Houston of Texas, then governor, refused point-blank to call a secession convention, sixty-one prominent proslavery men issued a private call. According to C. W. Ramsdell in his *Reconstruction in Texas,* half the counties held no elections, and in Travis County, where Austin, the capital, is located, only 342 votes were cast. Thus when the convention met on February 5, it was composed of proslavery elements, and the vote was 166 to 7 for secession. Houston refused to take the Confederate oath and was deposed. By 1863 when he was asked to run again, things were already in a bad state, with many families destitute and food riots beginning. Many Unionists had boldly taken the Union oath of allegiance and were advancing a peace movement for an early return to the Union.

From the start of war, armed anti-Confederate bands roamed up and down the state. Those from Zapata and Dimmit counties, near the Rio Grande, aroused particular alarm. On October 4, 1861, a Confederate general, Charles Anderson, was arrested for complicity. On the other hand, some northern and western counties, long harassed by Indian raids and attacking Kansas Jayhawkers, hoped that the Confederacy would do a better job of protecting them. When it failed to do so, their allegiance deteriorated.

Texas had many antiwar men. Quakers, Germans, Irish, and Mexicans—American citizens—were strongly opposed to the war. The Germans armed and resisted. There were pitched battles. In Fredericksburg, eighty miles west of Austin, a strong antislavery area, most of the men refused to enlist, hid in the hills, or fled to Mexico. A large body of armed Germans shot it out, through the entire war and on into Reconstruction days.

There were no Federal invasions of any consequence. Galveston was lost in October, 1862, but was recaptured in January and held until June 19, 1865, when General Gordon Granger landed and took over the state, freeing the slaves and nullifying all laws passed since 1861. Earlier the Federal troops had been kept out of Sabine Pass, but they held Brownsville throughout the war, and after capturing Fort Bliss and El Paso, controlled the Middle Rio Grande valley until the end. The chief effort of the North was to prevent the shipping of cotton and other goods to Mexico and vice versa. In August, 1862, rebel Corpus Christi was bombarded with shells containing whiskey, said to have caused great merriment wherever they fell, a civilized precedent not followed elsewhere.

At the time Granger took Galveston, 15,000 unpaid hungry Confederate troops swarmed into Austin, laid hold of everything movable and broke into the state treasury, making off with part of the funds. But Texas recovered rapidly, and during the period of military rule that lasted until 1869, many Southern families emigrated to the state to escape harsher conditions elsewhere, for Texas was still a frontier, a land of unhampered opportunities. It had suffered relatively little. The cattle business soon boomed, and great herds were driven north. Texas quickly put the war and the war within a war behind it and started toward its future greatness.

2. Virginia Split

West Virginia was born, if any single date and place can be given, on April 20, 1861, after Virginia walked out of the Union, in the room of delegate Sherrard Clemens in the Powhatan Hotel, Richmond. There thirteen delegates decided to call a western convention to form a new state of all-loyal pro-Union counties. If not antislavery *per se*, they had no interest in making war for the sole purpose of protecting the "peculiar institution"; their sympathies and personal interests were with the North.

They left Richmond the following day and called Unionist meetings in every northwest county. Delegates were named to a convention to be held in Wheeling, Ohio County, where Unionist sentiment was overwhelming. One-third of its population was foreign-born and against any war. There was published the *National Intelligencer*, edited by a bold antislavery Unionist, Archibald Campbell; and there prominent citizens favored setting up an independent government.

The call reminded the people that West Virginia had been denied equality in representation for half a century and was paying the bulk of the taxes with no corresponding benefits. Virginia's secession from the Union was the outcome of a deep-laid conspiracy hatched in the east for the selfish interests of the east alone, it was now said. Why should West Virginia be ruined by serving as a barrier to save the seaboard slave areas? Virginia's joining the Confederacy, following in the wake of South Carolina, the hotbed of political heresies and secession, would ruin the whole state; the idea of joining the cotton states was repugnant. The hour had struck to sever ties and remain under the protection of the federal government.

> Men of the Northwest: this is where Virginia stands today; this is how you stand; this has been your treatment; these the indignities you have suffered. Will you submit to a repetition of them? . . . Unite in this hour of common danger.

The eventual separation of West Virginia is a tangled, sordid story, but is an integral part of the war within a war. Though the Civil War was the immediate cause of the division, and slavery was the social lever, deep-seated sectional antagonisms—geographical, economic, and political—went back nearly a hundred years.

The two areas were simply not meant by nature to be one state. Only the blind chance of history, colonialism, and the surveyor's rod and chain had brought them under one government in the first place.

They were early populated by different ethnic groups, groups that thereafter had little contact or understanding. There were few roads and no railroads or canals between the two parts of the Old Dominion. Eastern Virginia was inhabited by Englishmen and Negroes, western Virginia by Germans, Scots, and Irish, with an English minority and a few French Protestants. They were thousands of miles apart in their racial, social, and institutional life.

The rugged Allegheny Mountains were partly responsible for the prolonged quarrels between the two sections, by setting off the mountain valleys from the eastern piedmont and the tidewater regions.

The Alleghenies consist of two major chains, the Blue Ridge mountains to the southeast and the main high ridges northeast, with the beautiful and fertile 300-mile-long Shenandoah Valley between. Then the only one feasible passage through either range was the James River and the Kanawha Valley. Western Virginia sloped from the Alleghenies to the Ohio River and bordered on Pennsylvania, Maryland, Ohio, and Kentucky. These were also her normal commercial outlets. Eastern Virginian commerce flowed northeast and to the Atlantic.

Western Virginia was highly individualistic, provincial, and isolated. Nearly all the counties—many walled in by high mountain spurs—were different from one another, topographically and otherwise. Only the rich East Panhandle counties were readily accessible to Piedmont Virginia, though more so to Washington and Maryland, for the rivers there empty into the Potomac. The North Panhandle was a narrow thumb of four counties between Pennsylvania and the Ohio River that geographically should properly have belonged to Pennsylvania. The Ohio River counties, and the nine Kanawha Valley counties were rough and topsyturvy. Another group of six counties, wild and sparsely settled, stretched along the southern part of the state from the Ohio to the Alleghenies. Each southwest mountain county was distinctive. The most important counties were the seventeen in the Monongahela River area below the North Panhandle.

By 1860 Virginia had a population of 1,800,000, the fifth state in the Union. Slaves numbered 490,000. Within what is now West Virginia, where 324,000 whites lived, were only 28,256 slaves. Thus West Virginia had twelve times as many whites as Negroes, East Virginia less than two to one. The Negroes were considered essential for tobacco farming, relatively little of which was grown in West Virginia. Yet tobacco production after the Civil War increased by a third in West Virginia and decreased a third in Virginia proper. Wool was a more important product, and West Virginia also produced most of Virginia's iron, coal, and other minerals.

For half a century the politically dominant slaveholders of the state, many of whom had publicly advocated a monarchical system, denied public improvements to the West and blocked the building of railroads and canals that would have tied the state together. Of the 1,579 miles of railroads in Virginia, only 361 miles were in the western counties. One real subsidy was granted in 1838 to the Baltimore and Ohio but even this was held up for more than ten years. It merely drew more trade away from Richmond to Baltimore. The rest of the trade came to be almost exclusively with Pittsburgh, Cincinnati, and Louisville, while there was almost none with Richmond. In 1856, more than a million people traveled between the Ohio Valley cities and Wheeling, a development further accelerated by the opening up of the Kanawha coal region.

Yet this flourishing western area had little say in running the Virginia government. Despite repeated protests by the western counties of inadequate representation, the tidewater slave planters controlled the state. Though western population growth had been rapid since the start of the century, no reforms were made until 1851, and these were not impressive. They did increase western representation in the senate and stated that all important offices were to be filled by popular vote, not by appointment. Still, the inclusion of nonvoting Negroes in population figures retained the imbalance, and representation was still in the ratio of four or five easterners to one westerner for the same number of freeholder voters. The freehold voting system disqualified most leaseholders, sharecroppers, mechanics, and tradesmen. Some eastern counties had scarcely two hundred white males, but had the same representation as western counties with greater wealth and production, which had thousands. The rotten borough system continued. Furthermore, Virginia slaveowners were given special tax benefits: all slaves under twelve years old were tax-free; adults at a flat assessment of $300 per capita. All other property was assessed at full value.

Up to the war no Senator had ever been elected from west of the Blue Ridge mountains, and before John Letcher, who, from their viewpoint, betrayed his western constituents, not one governor. All state employees were eastern men. No wonder that as early as 1846, western editorials advocated separation from the state, an attitude that spread widely, though largely allayed by the 1851 concessions.

The number of illiterate whites in the east far exceeded that in the west, which had a more extensive school system. The west was eager for schools but the slaveholding east clung to the mediaeval idea of colonial Governor Berkeley, that it was dangerous to allow the poor and ignorant to become enlightened.

When the hour for secession struck, the western counties faced a dilemma. Their loyalty to Virginia was still great, but isolated as they were from the rest of the state and the rest of the South, they could be overrun by Northern troops in a matter of days. Wheeling was only sixty-six miles from Pittsburgh. Pennsylvania would at once seize the northern panhandle. All economic and political ties were with the North, not with the reactionary slavocracy. Long before the blow fell, western leaders warned that secession of Virginia from the Union meant their ruin and that Federals would quickly take over their part of the state.

In April, 1861, the Wheeling *National Intelligencer* editorialized, "We are as powerless as an infant would be in the grasp of Hercules. They could crush us in a day." Where would they get protection? "From Richmond across the mountains? We might as well look to the moon for help."

But most westerners, confused and uncertain, did not want either secession or war. If the South complained of mistreatment by the North, no part of the Union and its people had been treated as badly by the ruling slaveowners of the Old Dominion as had West Virginia. The grievances of West Virginia against Virginia, said one newspaper, were ten times those of the South against the North.

Anti-Secessionist leader Francis H. Pierpoint told a Wheeling audience on May 23, 1860, that the undertaxation of slaves was costing the state, all told, nearly a billion dollars a year. In the east, $195,000,000 of property was wholly exempt from taxation, whereas the west had to pay through the nose, yet got nothing in return. The state debt had been increased by $30,000,000, all for improvements in the east. Incomes of slaveholders were not taxed a penny, but the poorest laborer had to pay over 10 per cent of his wages. "When the clerk dies or is sick, his wages cease, but the slaves go down as inheritance to the children of the owners."

But the people showed no passionate interest in setting up a new state. One writer believed that the pro-Union sentiment west of the mountains was 100 to 1. But others claimed the Secessionists outnumbered them 3 to 1. If anything, the few slaveholding counties seemed more pro-Union than some others, perhaps because the Unionists in such places were more vociferous. It was impossible, apparently, to get an objective appraisal of public opinion. "We have been hewers of wood and drawers of water for eastern Virginia long enough," said the *Intelligencer*. One paper said boldly it would take 100,000 bayonets from the Southern Confederacy to force western Virginia into a union with the cotton states. But the wet blanket of apathy lay over all, a sad sense of ruin and futility. Torn by conflicting emotions, most West Virginians simply didn't know what to do. They proceeded to bury their heads in the sand. Few volunteered for either side.

But newspapers began calling for a convention to set up a separate government.

> If the west is cut off from Ohio and Pennsylvania, grass will grow in every street next summer. . . . We are as much two people . . . even more, than those living on two sides of the Alps. . . . Nature made us part of Pennsylvania, the surveyor made us part of Virginia. . . . We hardly speak the same language. . . . If secession is pleasing and profitable let her go—Eastern Virginia—without the west.

"Dissolve this Union and hitch Virginia to the tail of a Southern Confederacy . . . and play patriot for King Cotton. I drop the pen, I cannot contemplate the picture," grieved one editor.

In answer to the call of the Powhatan Hotel rebels, four hundred and twenty-nine delegates from twenty-five West Virginia counties, mostly from the towns and cities—the deeper rural areas had only vague notions about the issues, or none at all—showed up in Wheeling on May 13, 1861.

This was the ten days before the state plebiscite on secession though actually Virginia authorities already had been acting as part of the Confederacy.

Most convention delegates at the original prewar state-wide convention in Richmond had voted against secession, but they were soon hemmed in by vigilantes, threatened with violence, or were being run out of the state. The West Virginia delegates were particularly harassed and threatened. A halter was flung over a tree in front of the boarding house where John Carlile, the western leader, was staying. The balconies at the convention were filled with a shouting mob. After Sumter the assemblage was stampeded, and a plebiscite to approve secession was set for May 23. The western delegates stood almost solidly against it. Two who switched over, Leonard Hall of Wetzel County and Samuel Woods of Barbour County, received such rough treatment on their return home that they fled to Richmond for most of the war.

The New York *Times* (May 10) prophesied grandiose results for the Wheeling convention: "a new Virginia, bright and fresh as the morning star will rise among the mountains of the west to shine with luster and glory for generations to come in a constellation of the Union. The thirteenth of May will be the beginning of grief to the revolutionists of Richmond." Only a mangled remnant of a once proud state would be left as an offering to the selfish hierarchies of Montgomery.

But aside from lambasting eastern slaveholders, the convention speeches were scarcely inspiring, and the body somehow failed to shine as the morning star. Mostly the endless harangues were dull, labored, and vacillating, or depressingly timid and unimaginative. It was a convention of bitter personal jealousies with little meeting of the minds or purposes. There was no solid support for dividing the state.

The delegates indulged in the most fatuous legalistic quibbling as to whether this body was in conformity with the Virginia and United States constitutions and laws? Actually, according to the Virginia constitution, only the General Assembly had the power to summon the people to a convention of this nature.

Jasper S. Wheat introduced resolutions denouncing secession from Richmond. Putting Virginia's militia into the hands of the

Confederacy violated the state constitution. But he wanted no *positive* action.

Was this merely a puffed-up mass meeting or, as the most fervent promoter of independent statehood, John S. Carlile, insisted, though with much legal falderal, a sovereign body that could do anything the sovereign people could do? Had the delegates come merely to deliberate or to form a new state? They had to act now or they would have to swear allegiance to the Confederacy. It was useless to cry peace when there was no peace.

William T. Willey, a Union man of long standing, though pro-slavery—the prince of vacillators and on both sides of the fence from hour to hour—shouted that Carlile's resolution was treason against the government of Virginia, of the United States, and the Confederate States of America! At the price of at least some mental indigestion, he both had his cake and ate it too.

Most delegates believed that any separation was illegal, so nothing was really decided, except to set up a central committee to prepare for a second convention in June. The New York *Times* prophecy had been a bit optimistic.

The war came closer. Northern and Confederate troops moved into various parts of the state. The Virginia plebiscite on May 23 for secession was apparently 6 to 1 in favor.

The central committee working for the June Wheeling convention sent out impassioned proclamations, with no mention of an independent state. It was hard to tell what the glowing words meant or why they were broadcast. Why all the uproar?

The June 11 convention was smaller, with only eighty-two delegates from twenty-seven counties. Twenty-five of these were state senators and house members. How the rest were chosen remains somewhat of a mystery. No open elections were held. Some were authorized by pro-Union county officials. Others merely got a few petition signers. But all took the oath to support the constitution of the United States and its laws and to refuse to accept the Virginia Secession Ordinance.

The biggest worry of the session seemed to be, not separation, but the state debt, which in equity, it was argued, since it had been assumed for east Virginia improvements, West Virginia should not assume even in part. But already, it was said, pressure had been brought by the Wall Street bondholders who were opposing recognition of any new government for West Virginia that would not recognize the existing debt. The Washington government, the delegates were told, would never disregard Wall Street orders.

Since no agreement on the debt was reached, the resolution to set up a new state was tabled for the entire session by a vote of 50 to 17. Carlile then proposed to reorganize the Virginia state government. The convention was to take the position that it represented not merely West Virginia, in itself doubtful, but all Virginia, then throw out all officeholders and appoint a new governor, name new officials, establish a new General Assembly and swear allegiance to the United States. The existing government, he argued, was a mere conspiracy. His ideas were adopted by unanimous vote. A special executive council of five to assist the new governor was established.

It was somehow denied that these drastic actions constituted separation or the establishment of a new state. But there is little doubt that the ruling clique had a plan and a timetable for independence that would avoid homegrown opposition and win recognition from the United States government.

F. H. Pierpoint (or, as he later called himself, Pierpont) was chosen Governor of "Virginia," and calls were sent out for the people to arm themselves against the corrupt oligarchy of Richmond. A new convention was to convene on August 6.

The new legislature of the new Virginia—at the beginning only three senators and twelve house delegates—was convened by Governor Pierpoint on July 2. Except for a few names, who composed it then or later, or what it did is largely unknown. Most deliberations were secret, and no records have survived. Opening business was the reading of the governor's message, a confused statement denouncing the betrayers in Richmond, which failed to make it clear whether this was really the government of Virginia or that of an independent new state.

Apparently the members spent considerable time debating whether they really were the legislature of Virginia. The *Intelligencer*, which could find out little else about what was going on, hoped they would make up their minds before adjournment. But the legislature did name Carlile and Willey as United States senators from Virginia, though Willey was against independent statehood and had refused to attend the second convention. His appointment was considered a bribe. The Morganstown *Star* said the leaders in Wheeling had been bought off by the New York bankers and the Secessionists.

The United States Senate, when asked to seat the two chosen senators, plunged into its own private underbrush of technicalities. Though the Virginia senators from Richmond had been expelled, this had occurred after the naming of Carlile and Willey. Furthermore, though relations had been severed with Virginia, the state General Assembly required a quorum of 79 in the House and 26 in the Senate. Also, since Lincoln contended that no Southern state had seceded (since that was unconstitutional), the Richmond Assembly remained the only bona fide legislature. Any de facto government was a revolutionary creation and had no status until recognized. "Why stick on the bank?" growled Senator Trumbull.

At this late date, the sophistries and petty legalisms hurled about sound ludicrous, the dancing of angels on a pin, all of it typical senatorial double talk, used not to enlighten but merely to confuse. But the administration wanted Carlile and Willey seated. They were seated—as Virginia, not West Virginia Senators.

The new rump Virginia legislature at Wheeling authorized separation, then sat as a convention on August 6. Again there was long-winded discussion whether the existing legislature really was a *Virginia* legislature. It was admitted that it was not legally such and that it was also illegal as a West Virginia legislature, since it had not come into being by the popular vote. Hence there was no legal way the convention could create an independent new state! A further absurd conclusion was reached:

that the secession of Virginia had been illegal, but that of West Virginia from the rest of the state was constitutional.

The delegates were touchy, confused, and irresolute. They veered from one extreme to the other between morning and afternoon. The same man sometimes introduced completely contradictory resolutions on the same day. Temporary officeholders held back because they wished first to be assured of jobs in any new state. No political or moral dignity was exhibited even by the so-called leaders. The delegates seemed afraid of their own theories and purposes, and the talkfest became a process of pulling petals off a daisy.

Once more the question of the debt was debated. Carlile suggested a practical solution: Virginia bonds were worth at best 30 cents on the dollar. Let West Virginia buy up her share and retire them. Some delegates were horrified by this betrayal of the bankers. Questions of slavery and minority rights also took up much time.

Stewart of north central Doddridge County said he had no instructions to set up a new state and doubted if any of the other delegates did. Since they had gone this far without popular sanction, let them dispense with the farce of an election and form a new state then and there. Leave it to the fall elections, argued some. Carlile insisted that it would be too late, that this was the last chance.

Step by step they moved on to considering the size and make-up of the new state. What size should it be? Carlile wished a small, compact state based on fairly solid pro-Union sentiments. Others wished to include an area from the top of the Alleghenies to the Ohio and also the eastern panhandle. Others wished to draw the boundaries to include the proslavery Shenandoah counties. One delegate wished to include a certain county because "it contained the grave of George Washington." The controversy took on acerbity. One session broke up in disorder and fist fights. The matter was finally referred to a Committee of Six.

Those who wished a large state seemed to be in the saddle. But should the counties have autonomy and right of self-determination? Or should the vote to establish the new state be decided by a state-wide majority? Even if a small, compact state was formed, only a fourth of the counties would or could vote, and some of these would vote against separation and against joining the Union. The larger the area included, the more counties would refuse to go along. It was finally voted that an over-all state vote would decide the fate of whatever counties were included.

The Committee of Six decided on a 39-county area, which would not include any large slaveholding counties. Seven additional counties were to be allowed to vote whether to become part of the new state. It was to be called Kanawha. A fair share of the original state debt was to be assumed. If any county official refused to open polls, two voting citizens anywhere could constitute themselves election commissioners to do so.

After heated debate, up until the last moment before adjournment, the ordinance to call for a constitutional convention was voted through 50 to 28.

The convention then sat the following day as the General Assembly of Virginia and ratified what the members had decided. Then, as the West Virginia legislature, it proceeded to implement the procedure, created offices, jobs, and salaries for its members. In such wise were all the legal (?) niceties observed.

Many Secessionists fled in terror from Wheeling and other points, vowing never to return until the "Goths and Vandals" were thrown out. Their property was confiscated, and the refugees carried bitter tales across the mountains of maltreatment. One crazy story was that Governor Pierpoint had arbitrarily divorced all wives remaining behind their fleeing husbands!

Governor Letcher of Virginia savagely denounced West Virginia's cruelty and oppression, though his part of the state had dealt even more cruelly with Union sympathizers. Later, he charged that the elections for the constitutional convention were fraudulent; the voters constituted "an army . . . of the reckless and abandoned, the dissolute and depraved, gathered from the purlieus of the cities and villages of the north and the floating scum of the western population."

It was true that known Secessionists were not allowed to vote and the returns were doctored. Anyone suspected of voting against the ordinance or being pro-Confederate was in danger of being violently assaulted. Most counties showed no opposition votes whatever, the remainder only a scattered handful. The biggest antistatehood vote was 18 in Marion County, versus a proseparation vote of 780. Even in Wheeling only a third of the normal vote was recorded. All told only 18,000 votes were cast in the entire state. The new West Virginia commonwealth was scarcely born in an atmosphere of democracy and freedom. By and large it was a revolution of local small farmers and artisans allied with Northern industrialists, traders, and financiers, plus local beneficiaries, against the landed gentry.

The elections were largely bayonet elections protected (or celebrated) by the militia or Northern soldiers, and where they were not present it was almost impossible to hold elections. In Cabell County a polling place, the only one, was set up "somewhere" by troops yet Cabell was an Ohio River county. Troops went into Kanawha County but were able to hold elections in only two precincts. They were able to hold open only two booths in Boone County, and barely got a toehold in a corner of Raleigh County to open a polling place. It was the same in Tucker County, where delegate Clarkson was elected by a vote of 39 in a single precinct. In Doddridge County, occupied by Federal troops and supposedly pro-Union, only a few voters turned out. Most of the 195 pro-Union votes in Hampshire County were cast by Union soldiers, of whom only 33 were Virginians. In Calhoun County, where all officials were pro-Confederate and no election could be held, the representative came with the signatures of 50 alleged voters. The Logan County delegate, actually a Kanawha man, for no one from the county would risk being a delegate, was seated on the petition of 15 persons from six families.

What the real sentiments of the West Virginia people were will probably never be known. The evidence seems to indicate that the vast majority either did not give a hoot or were too frightened to take sides. A large share of even pro-Union people simply did not want to see their state divided. How many were pro-Confederate can never be known. Many may have gone along with the independence movement because it was the less dangerous of the two alternatives. In any event it was still a minority conspiracy, abetted by Northern money and soldiers.

Even before separation was agreed upon, it had been all but impossible to get recruits to defend West Virginia. Three regiments were provided for, but of the 1,000 men actually recruited, only 150 were Virginians. The rest were from Ohio and Pennsylvania. In all the country towns, it was reported that "scores of great big, ugly, awkward, stand-up-and-call-mother-a-liar fellows" had been loafing around. All members of the largest militia company, an officer reported, were "secesh." Another officer wrote in that nearly all old-line officers were Rebels, "so how are we going to deal with the Secessionists?" A third reported that only "rebels and bushwackers" headed his outfit—"a burlesque"—and that in one county all elected officers were Rebels and Secessionists.

Thirty-seven delegates from thirty-one counties appeared at the constitutional convention in Wheeling on November 28, 1861. Their credentials, even from counties where no elections had been held, were scarcely questioned. "These are revolutionary times," said one ramrod of the convention; "The house is on fire, we cannot be technical." At this late date even the most technical delegates were merely quibblers, either concealing their frustrations or seeking to gloss over the cracks. Senator Willey was more blunt. "The county of Calhoun spurns our invitation . . . the county of Nicholas spurns our invitation. That is her own fault, sir. She might have been represented here; and if she sees it proper to stay at home and let us fix it for her, she has no right to complain."

The convention decided that the Shenandoah and East Panhandle counties could become part of West Virginia when and if they voted for annexation. Impractical, argued a Kanawha County delegate; a Union Army would first have to take over. Some wished to deny the vote to everybody not known to be pro-Union. In general, except for the leaders, pro-Union people belonged to the poorer classes, but even many of them, it was alleged, had helped friends and kin serving in the Confederate army, as indeed had nearly every delegate present. Many had been and were committing treason with as little compunction as shooting squirrels. To limit the suffrage would endanger everybody's voting rights.

But delegates feared that if all were permitted to vote by secret ballot, there was real danger the Secessionists actually might win, almost certainly so in the border counties, and that even in many other counties Secessionists were probably in the majority. One delegate said he had been in McDowell County in June and had found quite a number of men there were pro-Union in their hearts, but they dared not say so. So outspoken and pessimistic were the discussions that the proceedings have never been published.

In general the delegates showed more excitement and passion over the name "Kanawha" than the serious issues. One objection, a true one, was that it was hard to spell. Sentimental speeches were made about the name "Virginia," but one delegate said bitterly that it had meant "only oppression and outrage" for West Virginians. The name "West Virginia" was finally adopted by a 2 to 1 vote.

The delegates, often with heated debate, finally worked out a constitution more liberal than that of the Old Dominion; it provided for popular education, universal white male suffrage, secret ballot, and internal improvements. After angry debate, resolutions to abolish slavery were set aside, except for a clause introduced by a Methodist preacher, prohibiting slaves or free Negroes from ever entering the state! It was one of the greatest ironies of history that in this colossal struggle, with its mountains of dead, of which the Negro was a main cause, so few peo-

: *43* :

ple either North or South gave a tinker's damn about the fate of the Negro or his rights.

The constitution was submitted to the voters in April, 1862, and adopted by 20,622 to 40. More than a third of the vote was cast by the four North Panhandle counties. Two other counties, the largest, brought the total up by a good majority of all votes cast, so that six counties decided the fate of the new state. At least nine counties held no elections. In strong Secessionist counties the pro-Union vote was given out as unanimous. One United States colonel had been instructed, he said, to let no one vote against the new constitution. One estimate was that at least half the counties were against separation (though not necessarily Secessionist). The new state was formed, as Greeley put it in his *American Conflict*, on the assumption that only the loyal people of a state constitute the state. In other words, it was one-party rule, the only kind of rule possible in a revolutionary situation, though Governor Pierpoint hotly denied that it was a revolutionary proceeding. He had insisted on the complete legality of every step. Certainly an appearance of legality was maintained.

Following the election count, the West Virginia legislature of forty-one members smoothly converted itself back into the *Virginia* legislature, duly put its stamp of approval on the outcome, and authorized the new state. At once it reverted to being the *West Virginia* legislature. It was like a boss doubling as his own office boy, putting his cap off and on. It adopted the constitution, per popular vote, and petitioned for admission to the Union. There is no record that anybody smiled at all this hocus-pocus.

The admission resolution came before Congress in May. One humorous aspect was that the proslavery advocate, Senator Willey, long opposed to statehood, now emerged as its most fervent supporter. His conversion was greater than that of Paul, one Senator mocked. Debate dragged on, and Willey led for prompt action. He said that West Virginia stood with her heart bleeding, all her industrial and commercial interests prostrate; if decision were long delayed, Union men would have to flee from the state. But whether West Virginia was standing, prostrate, or fleeing, the quibbling continued.

In contrast, Carlile, who had once declared that there was scarcely a dissenting vote in West Virginia, now told the Senate that the convention in no way represented the people of the state. Back in Wheeling, he was called a Judas Iscariot, and the General Assembly called for him to resign.

The farcical United States Senate debate over legality and constitutionality went on, interrupted by a long feud with Senator Charles Sumner over forcing the state to abolish slavery as the price of admission, a step finally taken. Amazingly, in the Senate bill, fifteen additional counties beyond the expanded number included in the petition for admission, were included—counties with nearly 32,000 slaves. One West Virginian commented that it would be tying two cats together by the tail.

Newspapers, North and South, were almost as pompous about the legality of the matter, though the Northern press was inclined to support admission on the sheer grounds of expediency. The *Times*, despite the constitutional clause guaranteeing debt payment, was particularly worried over the innocent Virginia bondholders. A few papers insisted there were many loyal Unionists in the rest of Virginia; it was not right to carve up the state while they were bound hand and foot by the rebellion.

The Senate finally authorized admission by a 3 to 1 vote, but the House put the matter off until December. And so West Virginia had to keep on bleeding for another half-year, despite the exigencies of war.

The House then plunged into its own brand of quibbling. The war thundered on and the House thundered on with its small-calibre rattle. It did produce, for reasons unknown, some amusing contradictions which at that late date had little meaning. It was asserted that the creation of the new state was scarcely democratic! More than 80,000 people, a majority, in the counties actually voting, had never expressed their desire for independence; nor had even a majority of the counties. Ten other counties had never voted on the constitution. Still other counties were so obviously part of eastern Virginia that it was improper to force them to swear allegiance to a government in which they had no participation. Furthermore as late as May, only 14,824 persons had gone to the polls, not an enthusiastic or representative turnout.

The chief backer of the resolution for admission, Congressman John A. Bingham of Ohio, argued that the refusal of qualified voters to go to the polls had no bearing on the matter. The loyal minority of the new state had created it and were the only ones properly qualified to form a government. Only those taking the oath of allegiance to the United States should be considered members of any state, have a right to vote or hold office.

Other speakers amused themselves by noting that the local legislature, posing as that of all Virginia and authorizing partition, was the same one claiming to be that of West Virginia and petitioning for admission of part of the state as a new state. Stephens of Pennsylvania admitted the legal hypocrisy. He did not believe that admission was in the least constitutional, but he was voting for it because of the absolute power vested in the North by the laws of war. Noell of Wisconsin also believed that it was unconstitutional, but these were revolutionary times; they could not afford to split technical hairs. West Virginia was admitted by a vote of 96 to 55.

Before signing the bill, Lincoln asked for written opinions from his cabinet. Was it constitutional? Was it expedient? In these relatively unrelated, even contradictory questions, the cabinet was equally divided. The Attorney General said it was both unconstitutional and inexpedient. West Virginia owed its origin to necessity, not law, a revolutionary procedure. It was attempted *secession*, not covered under existing forms of law.

Lincoln signed the bill with a casuistical explanation. The consent of the Virginia legislature was constitutionally required, and a body claiming to be such a legislature had given its consent. It had been sad that a majority of voters of Virginia did not participate. But it was universal procedure to give no legal consideration whatever to those who do not choose to vote! Obviously, only those choosing to do so constituted the political power of the state!

He next considered expediency. Whatever helped restore national authority was the most expedient. The North could scarcely dispense with the aid of West Virginia and much less afford to have her against the Union. The confidence and cooperation of the loyal men who had set up the new government could not be strained by breaking faith with them. Second, since Congress had imposed abolition of slavery as a condition of admission, that much more slave territory would be made free.

It had been argued that this reluctance had been demonstrated in fear of setting up a precedent, but, he added, with sublime disregard for history (and with considerable sophistry) a measure made expedient by war was no precedent for times of peace. Some had said we were accepting West Virginia's secession because it was our secession, and he added slyly, that there was still difference enough between secession *against* the constitution and the secession *in favor of* the constitution. He took up his pen and signed.

The constitution, with amended antislavery clause, was ratified in 48 counties by a vote of 18,862 to 514. And so, on June 30, 1863, West Virginia became the thirty-fifth state, and Virginia permanently lost a third of her territory. It was a conspiracy, a revolution, and an act of war, a result obtained in good part by Northern bayonets. But the new entity came into the Union not so much as a state as a military and political colony. Perhaps it represented the will of the people. We shall, in all likelihood, never know. That it did correspond to the wishes of a large share of the people is obvious. To this day, large parts of it are destitute. Yet in some ways, it was the most tangible and the most enduring achievement of the war within a war.

3. The Dark Lantern

A pacifist has been defined as a man who believes in peace in peacetime. The Southern peace-lovers were people of a different stamp. They organized and worked for peace in wartime, some risking their lives and all they had. In the eyes of Southern patriots, they were the vilest traitors. In the eyes of Northerners, they were true patriots. Most, of course, were not really pacifists but citizens fighting for the Union on Southern soil. But many more wanted no part of the war one way or the other. In any case, many were devoted men with a superior moral concept of human life. They may well have been the real heroes of the South, and of course real heroes are often unsung.

Much of the war within a war was conducted by secret peace societies, which soon riddled the whole South. These dark lantern groups, meeting clandestinely in barns or in field and forest, kept resistance alive, plotted sabotage, and arranged for escapes to the North. They were very much involved in the Know-Nothing secret societies, in turn modeled on the Masonic Order, which had been widespread in all states for ten years before the war, so that a large share of the population were well educated in dark lantern methods, how to operate, escape detection, and strike out against authority.

The first anti-Secessionist peace society—The Peace and Constitutional Society—was started in Van Buren County, Arkansas, in the fall of 1861. Members took an oath, utilized signs and passwords, were pledged to aid each other, encourage army desertion, promote enlistment with Union forces and help Federal invaders of Arkansas soil. They were forbidden to give aid to any

Confederate soldier or official of the Conscription Bureau. Any disloyalty or disclosure by a member was punishable by death. The group enjoyed regular money contributions, and its members were well armed.

Army agents soon discovered that the order had 700 members in the northwest counties and 1,700 in the state. On October 29, Adjutant-General Edmund Burgevin, C.S.A., had twenty-seven arrested and sent to Little Rock for trial.

Several months later Governor Rector informed President Davis and Secretary of War Benjamin that he was still holding the twenty-seven. One hundred and eleven more had been arrested, but on the insistence of local citizens, they were allowed to enlist in various commands.

Colonel Solon Borland sent two infantry companies into the northwest counties where local home guards had already captured more disloyalists. Forty were sent to Little Rock for trial. Eighty more were held in local jails. Fifty-seven, "mostly illiterates," claimed they had been fooled and asked to enlist. Most, being unfit for duty, were taken on as teamsters and mechanics. Forty others, one a state legislator, had escaped the dragnet, and joined the Union army at Rolla, Missouri.

The Peace Society, a more widespread organization, active in at least six states, also flourished in Arkansas, having spread there from Alabama and East Tennessee early in 1862. Many Confederate soldiers became "contaminated" by this group. Units known to have such members were rushed off to the front lines. As a result, the Society penetrated deeply into much of the Confederate army, especially around Cumberland Gap.

In central Alabama, Colonel Jefferson Faulkner of the Eighth Confederate Cavalry allowed himself to be initiated into the order to learn its secrets. From such initiated agents comes much of what is known of the organization, for no records were kept and no organized lodges were maintained. Each member was an independent dissevered link in a perfect chain—a society without officers, a community without available membership lists.

Grips, signs, and passwords varied from locality to locality, but the usual signs of recognition were:

1. Salute with right hand, thumb pointing backwards.

2. The person saluted, if one of the faithful, then clasped his hands, knuckles of the left down, those of the right up.

3. Both looked each other in the eye, and the first person tapped his right foot with a stick, then broke it and tossed the pieces over his left shoulder.

4. If in a group or crowd, the signal was three careless slaps on the right leg.

5. In prison, repetition of the word "Washington" four times brought quick release, if the guard was one of the faithful.

6. If challenged by a Federal picket or sentinel, the password was "Jack," the answer, "All right, Jack, pass on with your goose quills."

7. In battle, the gun butt was placed on the right hip, barrel at a 15-degree angle to the right, then brought to left-shoulder arms according to Scott's regulations.

After the due signs, the following dialogue was exchanged.

Q. "What is that?"
A. "A grip."
Q. "A grip of what?"
A. "A constitutional peace grip."
Q. "Has it a name?"
A. "It has."
Q. "Will you give it to me?"
A. "I did not so receive it, neither can I so impart it."
Q. "How will you impart it?"
A. "I will letter it with you."
Q. "Letter it and begin."
A. "Begin you."
Q. "No, you begin."
A. "Begin you."

The purpose was to organize an anti-Davis party; overthrow the existing state governments by attacking home guards and Secessionists, and, finally to break down the Confederate Govern-

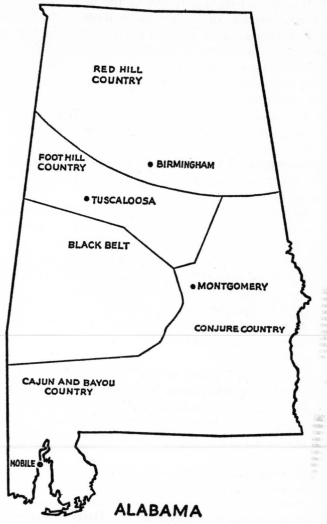

RED HILL
COUNTRY

FOOT HILL
COUNTRY

● BIRMINGHAM

● TUSCALOOSA

BLACK BELT

● MONTGOMERY

CONJURE COUNTRY

CAJUN AND BAYOU
COUNTRY

MOBILE ●

ALABAMA

Alabama. Regional areas. Armed resistance throughout
Red Hill country spread to foothills and bayous, and part
of Cajun and "Conjure" country.

ment and compel the authorities to make peace by refusing all support. Some wanted to return to the Union on a program of negotiated settlement. Others wished the South to offer unconditional surrender. The organization was usually led by prominent personages who took the oath of allegiance to the United States. The *Mobile Advertiser* sneered that they were whimpering for peace and reconstruction, and the *Richmond Enquirer* said their patriotism had been corrupted by love of cotton. Others said that they had been corrupted by Grant's soldiers when Vicksburg fell.

To substantiate the latter statement, by May, 1863, the peace movement was in full swing around Vicksburg and Natchez. Members managed to get on nearly every draft board and handed out furlough passes wholesale to deserters. The organization boasted that the defeats of both Missionary Ridge and Vicksburg were its own doing, which was, of course, ridiculous.

In Randolph County, Alabama, two-thirds of the people belonged to the Peace Society, including the commander of the state reserves, army officers, an ex-state senator, a prominent Methodist minister, justices of the peace, and other officeholders, conscription officers, doctors (who declared men unfit for the draft) and a large share of the soldiers.

Discontent soon took on tangible political shape. In the midsummer of 1863 elections in Alabama, Peace Party candidates won right down the line, and six pro-Unionists were sent to the Confederate Congress in Richmond. Even the original firebrand, Yancey, was defeated by an anti-Secessionist. Among those sent to Richmond was William R. W. Cobb of Jackson County, a man constantly in touch with the Federals, who passed through their lines freely. Davis' Congress angrily expelled him.

The Peace Society maintained lines of communication between Northerners, the Tennessee Unionists, and in Alabama as far south as Talapoosa County. Later it spread to all counties, particularly in the southeast. General Gideon J. Pillow ordered the arrest of Major May and all officers connected with the society for suspicious actions favoring the enemy. "Exterminate the

Peace Society in all Alabama!" was the military watchword. But, though arrests were numerous, its activities were not successfully curbed.

In South Alabama and West Florida, General J. H. Clayton's forces, sent in especially to round up deserters and put an end to the Peace Society and another secret subversive body—Heroes of America—found his own troops honeycombed with disloyal members. Seventy men schemed for a mass uprising on Christmas Day but were arrested and sent to Mobile for court martial. A few weeks later more were arrested. Those jailed said that since they had nothing, they had nothing to fight for. All of Clayton's soldiers were believed to be unreliable and were sent to General Leonidas Polk in Mississippi to be distributed among trusted veteran troops. This spread the poison more rapidly.

In northeast Mississippi, secret meetings were held to devise ways of evading the law, and a regular underground developed there helped many to escape across the border. Professional pilots, "who could course it from point to point through the forests, with the unerring instinct of a panther or the catamount or aborigines," led whole squads to enlist in the Northern army. From the Ohio River to the Gulf the password *Taisez-vous* was answered by *Oui, oui*. According to Reverend John H. Aughey, passwords and countersigns were never discovered during the entire war. In Tishomingo County, where he had taken refuge after being driven out of Choctaw County, the password was more often "The Union Forever," or "Liberty and Union now and forever, one and inseparable."

By 1862 Confederate army agents began ferreting out, persecuting, and punishing peace advocates. Vigilantes also operated. But most Unionists had a rude arbor in the woods where they slept at night or took refuge when danger loomed. Fires were lit on hilltops to call meetings or communicate warnings. Locations were disguised by such agreed-upon names as "Mount Sinai," "Nebo," "Pisgah," "Horeb," "Hermon."

At ten o'clock one night in April, Reverend Aughey saw

flames rising high from Horeb and Hermon. It was an urgent call. Silent gliding figures slipped through the dark, and by midnight more than ninety men and women were present. A Confederate searching party appeared close by. Two Unionists and four soldiers were killed.

Shortly after, Reverend Aughey and a hundred others were ordered to face court martial on June 1, 1862. He urged all to attend and defend themselves. But, learning they would likely be killed by lurking Confederate cavalry and vigilantes, all decided to escape to the Federal garrison at Farmington. En route, at Rienzi, Aughey was overjoyed to see the Stars and Stripes in pursuit of Confederates fleeing from Corinth. He settled there, but went back and forth through the lines, and became a buying agent, working to get cotton from Southern speculators for the North. He also had agents getting information about Confederate forces. As a result the Federals were often able to surprise and capture soldiers at strong points.

Later, as the Union cavalry scoured every corner of north Mississippi, the welcome to Federal forces, wrote a Captain S. L. Phillips, was genuine and heartfelt. Tears flowed down the cheeks of the men as well as of the women. Members of the society were duly honored and favored by the Federals.

Particularly prevalent among soldiers was the organization Heroes of America which, apparently as early as 1862, flourished in Alabama, North Carolina, southwest Virginia, and Tennessee. According to the Raleigh *Standard*, one local founder was North Carolina's State Auditor, Henderson Adams. It was organized in most of Virginia in the fall of 1863, by a Horace Dean, of North Carolina. However, its existence was not discovered by the Virginia authorities until 1864.

General R. T. Nicholls (2nd Louisiana Brigade, who ran the Conscript Bureau), investigating it in southwest Virginia, a solidly anti-Secessionist area, said it had been set up originally at the suggestion of the Northern authorities, and that its main headquarters were north of the Federal lines. Certainly members were allowed to pass freely through Union lines, and the North offered its members draft exemption, property protection, and participation in future distribution of confiscated Confederate property.

The order was probably started, certainly abetted, by the Federal Secret Service to undermine the morale of the Southern soldiery. In the trial of one member, it was alleged that the oath of this society had been taken by both Lincoln and Secretary of War Stanton. (Report, 42nd Cong., 1st Sess. 1468:227.) This seems improbable.

When it was safe to do so, members wore a red and white cord or ribbon—a biblical reference to Rahab—and were known as "The Red Strings." The dialogue exchanged was:

> "*These are gloomy times.*"
> "Yes, but we are looking for better."
> "*What are you looking for?*"
> "A red and white cord."
> "*Why a cord?*"
> "Because it's safe for us and our families."

Identification was also established by uttering the word "Three." The answer was "Days."

The group promoted desertion, aided and protected deserters, helped prisoners to escape, assisted Northern spies and reported Confederate troop positions and movements. Members were pledged to help the North and defeat the Confederacy in every way possible.

Not until 1864 did the Confederacy get around to sending in detectives to ferret out Virginia members of the Heroes of America. Pretending to be hiding out from arrest, such agents managed to win confidence, get names, grip signs, and passwords. Nearly everybody in six counties was discovered to be a member. The surprise killing of General John H. Morgan, C.S.A., was attributed to the Heroes.[1] But there was no use arresting any members; no court anywhere would convict them,

---

[1] Which again seems improbable, at best.

because of either sympathy or fear of reprisals. Many members actually held public office as policemen, judges, and sheriffs.

To meet the tense situation, the army declared martial law in all southwest Virginia. But the Federals were moving down, and three days after they attacked, the local Unionists marched through Lee County on the Tennessee and Kentucky border, openly with drums and fifes and flying the Stars and Stripes.

4. AWOL

Captain Daniel Ellis, one pilot among hundreds, who had found a new profession in Tennessee, Alabama, and other states—claimed he had guided 10,000 men through the lines to join the Federal army in Kentucky and Tennessee. Many were Confederate deserters. The loyalty of all East Tennessee soldiers in the Confederate army, wherever stationed, was doubtful. Even Confederate General G. B. Crittenden, whose brother was a Union general, was suspected of disloyalty and was believed to have caused the disaster in East Tennessee that led to the death of General F. K. Zollicoffer. Many Southern troops disliked serving under him, and he was relieved of command in 1862.

Among others, Captain Robert W. Boone, grandson of Daniel Boone, was a Northern secret agent, who served in at least eight different Confederate regiments as a private or officer, and who ran a Northern spy organization in four states. He helped deserters and rescued and personally piloted captured Union officers back to the North.

In May, 1863, a month before Gettysburg, a new Texas recruit joined his outfit, the 4th Texas, in Virginia. The conditions then existing indicate why many men deserted. For officers and fine leaders it was still something of a play war. Ladies on horseback came out to enjoy dress reviews. But on such occasions, as in the Texas outfit, many barefoot and ragged men had to be kept out of the line. The volunteer realized the meagerness of Southern resources when he received two haversacks, miserably weak and sleazy, made out of thin cotton cloth. He told how shortly afterward, without rhyme or reason, his unit was marched, 10,000 of them, through rain and mud and fell exhausted in a heap like so many tired hounds on the wet roadside, without warm food. At daylight they were all marched back sixteen miles over the same road to their old camp, then on to another place half a mile from Culpeper. "This marching and counter marching is what military authorities call making a demonstration . . . a tiresome and monstrous business." Many deserted.[1]

By August, 1863, Major-General Gideon J. Pillow of Tennessee who, in 1861, had rushed to Richmond before Secession to offer the Confederacy 50,000 troops, reported that no more conscripts could be obtained in his state, and desertions were increasing. In all, 31,000 Tennesseeans enlisted in the Union army, while 4,000 fought the Confederacy from inside the state. From 5,000 to 10,000 Confederate troops had to be diverted from the front in order to keep the people down and try to prevent resistance, sabotage, and uprisings.

Real trouble began brewing in northern Alabama even before the Confederate Congress started debating conscription. In various counties, strong, armed, outlaw bands went into regular encampments, and groups of hundreds of deserters roamed through Franklin and Lawrence counties. In January 19, 1862, investigator Robert P. Blount informed Secretary Benjamin that he believed the outlaws in two counties planned to free prisoners at Tuscaloosa, where many dissidents were held.

Early in 1862 Federal forces invaded. On April 11, Brigadier-General Ormsby M. Mitchell entered Huntsville, and General Albert Sidney Johnston, commanding for the Confederacy in the West, had to retreat to Corinth. From then on Federal troops crisscrossed the entire north of the state, accompanied by armed bands of brigands, vagabonds, deserters, draft resisters, and ardent Unionists—robbing, burning, destroying, raping, and murdering. Ardent Secessionists were sure to be attacked and their

---

[1] Desertions from *both* armies, it should be noted, were enormous, and throughout the whole war. Record keeping was in its infancy.

property destroyed. Sometimes they were captured and sent to Northern prisons. Hordes of people were driven out of the area. A Confederate Major-General, Jeremiah Clemens of Huntsville, actually joined the Union army.[2] George W. Lane, who had never lowered the Stars and Stripes from his house, was named a judge.

Even in unoccupied counties, the conscription law could scarcely be enforced, and resisters freed imprisoned deserters. The few conscripts that were gathered in promptly deserted. Alabama draftees should be sent to Virginia or elsewhere at once, said one army officer, where it will not be so easy for them to get home. The 3rd Alabama Reserve Regiment deserted en masse.

It was the practice of many men to allow themselves to be sent back to the front, where they laid hands on all the guns and equipment they could and came back home. Some did this as many as four times. Officers who got in their way were killed.

On July 28, 1863, General Pillow [3] reported 8,000 to 10,000 deserters in the north Alabama mountains, and said there were not enough Confederate soldiers in all Alabama to round up deserters. It was useless to capture the runaway hillbilly and sand-mountain conscripts. No court would punish them; the army could not use them and dared not shoot them. The outlaws ruled the roosts, for, aside from deserters and resisters, about the only people left at home were those exempted; the lame, the halt and the blind, teachers and preachers, etc.

Even in Alabama's southeastern Harrison and Florida counties, forces had to be dispatched to stamp out Unionism and treason, and drive out bands of deserters, "Tories," and runaway slaves. A few deserters were arrested, but they were largely released at gun point.

---

[2] He was a prewar writer of romances and an anti-Secession delegate to the Secession Convention.

[3] General Pillow, it should be noted, was the hopeless incompetent who lost Fort Donelson to U. S. Grant. He seems not to have improved when transferred.

On the eve of battles there were always heavy desertions. Numerous soldiers crawled over to the enemy lines at night. Carl Schurz, who had a Federal command at Mission Rock, reported that in the morning before the battle the spaces between the headquarters tents were so jammed with deserters he could hardly get through. They brought information about troops, ammunition, food supplies, and intended movements.

Several thousand of General John B. Hood's men, whose forces were honeycombed with Heroes of America members, deserted, took the Federal oath of allegiance and dispersed to their homes. Obstruction of the draft became steadily worse. It became dangerous for Confederates to travel in many parts of the state; and in most places courts could not function except with armed protection.

On the North Carolina seaboard, people were infuriated by lack of adequate coast defenses and the official burning of their cotton to keep it out of enemy hands. After the Conscription Act, disloyalty and plotting spread everywhere. Prominent leaders in the state openly claimed that the law was unconstitutional. It was not on record that W. W. Holden advocated desertion, but he was bitterly opposed to conscription: "The idea of sending free citizens of the state from their homes to camps of instruction against their will, to be trained to fight for liberty, was, to say the least, absurd. The war should have been a voluntary one."

In October, 1862, Governor Vance wrote Davis that it would be exceedingly difficult to execute the President's draft call, even if he did not have the problem of West Point generals who, knowing little of human nature, rode rough-shod over the people, dragged them from their homes, and *consigned* them to strange regiments and strange commanders.[4] He had to decline a task which would certainly fail. He added, "The waters of in-

---

[4] Presumably they should have put them in familiar regiments with their own commanders! This was a recurring problem throughout the war, because state politicians wanted just that!

subordination are beginning to surge more angrily than ever." Many openly declared that they didn't want another conscript to leave the state. Others said it (the state) would not have labor enough to support the women and children. "Thousands are fleeing from the eastern counties to the centre and west, to devour the very short crops and increase the prospects of starvation." On top of this, Governor Letcher of Virginia was threatening to cut off salt. A month later Vance wrote to state that it was his duty to protect some forty persons seized by Major-General W. H. French, Third Army Corps. Their first right was a trial. In January he protested to the Confederate Secretary of War against appointing outside conscription officers to enforce a law both harsh and odious, ". . . strangers to all positions in this State, North Carolina." To put such men over troops was going to cause bad feeling.

The month following he was complaining for the second time of the quartering of broken-down cavalry horses in the northwest counties, which were devouring the substance of a people already threatened with famine. Unless they were soon removed, he would call out militia and drive them out of the state.

In December, 1863, he denounced Confederate troops in the state for stealing, pilfering, burning, and sometimes murderous conduct, and asked for demotion of officers responsible, with a few shootings as examples, or he would have to call out the militia and carry out actual war against them.

In spite of Davis' abolition of *habeas corpus*, Chief Justice Richmond Pearson never once denied the writ for the release of conscripts, deserters, or traitors, and Governor Vance ordered the militia not to rearrest them or seize anybody except by court order.

Captured deserters constituted a dilemma. To bring them into the courts could lead to the Conscription Act being declared unconstitutional, something Supreme Court Justice Pearson was just itching to do. To shoot them by a drumhead court martial, or without a trial, would mean nobody's life would be safe.

In December, 1862, a band of North Carolina men, women,

and children, said to be pro-Unionist, raided Salisbury, near Marshall, the seat of western Madison county, to get salt. They plundered stores and other property en route. Captain J. A. Keith of the 64th North Carolina rounded them up, put ropes around the necks of the women and had them flogged. Thirteen old men and boys were shot. One fifteen-year-old was wounded and brought in with his broken arm dangling. His mother pled for his life, but Keith whipped out his pistol and shot him in the head. Bitterness rose to fever pitch. The governor asked Under Secretary of War Jasper A. Seddon to remove Keith for brutality and court-martial him, adding that he (the governor), would follow him to the gates of hell and hang him. But Keith was acquitted on the grounds that he had merely been carrying out the orders of his superior, General D. H. Hill. After the war, Keith was rearrested, escaped from jail, and fled to California.

At the front, North Carolinians were soon deserting at the rate of fifty a week. Whole squads left, taking their arms. Regiments were being decimated worse than by a battle. More than a hundred men from the 58th North Carolina deserted to the Federals as well as large numbers from Tennessee and Georgia regiments.

A concerted letter-writing campaign, perhaps organized by the Heroes of America, was carried on to discourage the troops at the front. Tatum quoted North Carolina letters from the *War of the Rebellion*, the 130 volumes of the official records of the Union and Confederate armies:

"You said you hadn't anything to eat," Martha Revis wrote her husband, "I wish you were here to get some beans for dinner. I have plenty to eat as yet. . . . The people is all turning to Union here since the Yankees has got Vicksburg. I want you to come home as soon as you can after you gits this letter. . . . The conscripts is all at home yet, and I don't know what they will do with him. The folks is leaving here, and going North as fast as they can."

A hired hand wrote: "I am well, and is right strait out for the

Union, and I'm never going in the strife any more, for I am for the Union forever and ever, amen . . . Your brother till death. Hurrah for the Union! Hurrah for the Union!"

By 1863 it was no stigma to be a deserter. Quite the contrary, for leaders who had been ardent promoters of secession, now openly urged soldiers to desert, saying the war was lost, and demanding an end to it.

Hundreds of deserters were already boldly living at home and growing crops. More were streaming home. When halted and asked for their furloughs, they patted their guns, "This is my furlough." The conscription officers turned away "as peaceable as possible." In groups of as many as fifty to five hundred deserters forced their way across guarded bridges and roads and on to ferries. They ate well, too, because of either sympathy or fear.

Back at home, those driven into outlawry terrorized pro-Confederates and destroyed their property, continually threatening to bring in the enemy. They threatened the families of officers attempting to arrest them with knife and torch. Strong outlaw bands operated in Greenville County and in Pickens and Spartanburg counties of South Carolina, along the North Carolina line. They had leaders, spies, and danger signals. Every woman and child was a watch and guard for them, a captain reported. The deserters and draft-resisters had regular reunion points and a little northeast of the Greenville courthouse, they set up a strong log blockhouse. Soldiers sent to apprehend them often deserted en masse, as for instance the 16th South Carolina Volunteers under General C. H. Evans.

Governor Vance shifted ground when all this lawlessness of the deserter bands got out of hand, for in the mountain counties all travel had come to a halt. Burning and plundering were soon terrorizing a large part of the state, and he had to call for Confederate army aid.

In his 1864 message to the General Assembly, he said:

> Bands of lawless men . . . swarm in the mountain frontier, murdering, burning and destroying . . . a system of cruelty, at

which humanity shudders. . . . Deserters representing almost every state of the Confederacy infest the swamps and marshes of many counties. . . . In some places they muster in such forces as to almost amount to the suspension of civil authority, aided and protected as they are by relatives and friends.

All efforts to abate the nuisance by offers of pardon had failed. The iron hand of force had become necessary. In addition, part of the home guard in interior counties, and some civil officials, too, had deserted. Many had fled to the enemy.

In Virginia all males between 18 and 35 who deserted or failed to report for the draft were ordered shot. Sometimes it worked the other way. A "General" Floyd, at the head of bad, bold, disappointed men, plundered and looted on all sides. Anyone criticizing the resisters had his home burned, or was waylaid, beaten, or murdered. All the best people of the area were completely demoralized, and by fall a new "state" of "Southwest Virginia" was organized. Brigades of deserters, headed by an elected "general," provided its defense.

In the army itself, it was claimed, most men in the 22nd and 54th Virginia Regiments were Heroes of America. Most of the 22nd deserted to the Union army. By January, 1865, General Cadmus Wilcox reported fifty men deserting every day.

Governor Brown of Georgia, who fought the Conscription Acts throughout, wrote Davis that his legislation was subversive of Georgia's sovereignty, unfair, oppressive, and uncalled for. He refused to cooperate with conscription agents and would not permit *any* state employee to be removed from the state.

As early as 1862, the Secretary of War had reported that more than half of Georgia's volunteers from the northeast counties were back at home without leave—this even before the Conscription Act. Armed bands of deserters and their sympathizers soon roamed about, freeing prisoners and existing on plunder. Fifty ringleaders were finally arrested by the state militia; two hundred men were sent back to their units, and two thousand deserters were driven out of the state. Many soon came back, for they were protected by the people, even though, by 1863, following bad crops, north Georgia was close to starvation. Deserters believed they had been fighting, not their own battles, but those of the politicians, officers, and planters. Many became avowed members of the Peace Society.

When the draft age was raised to 45, Governor Brown became really angry: "No act of the government of the United States," he said, "had ever struck a blow at constitutional liberty so foul as has been stricken by the Conscription Acts." He demanded a cessation of conscription in Georgia. The people of his state had entered the war as free men and intended to emerge from it free men. He demanded the right to withhold or withdraw any and all Georgian troops from the army. After Chickamauga, a nominal Confederate victory, he insisted that Georgia's twelve-month volunteers—held overtime in service—be returned home to attend to their crops and businesses. When this was refused, he said that since the government had broken faith with the soldiers, it was unlikely more troops would be contributed by Georgia. By the time of Sherman's invasion, Brown, more contemptuous than ever of Davis' pleas for help, furloughed all militia forces. If Davis wished Georgians to fight for him, let him send for those still in General Lee's forces.

By 1864 there were many more deserters, many of them broken, spiritless men. George W. Pepper, who was with Sherman, described them. "As we drew nigh to the first town, we were met by a party of the most miserable-looking group I have ever beheld. . . . Bare-footed and bare-legged, with scarcely as many tatters hung around them as covered their naked limbs . . . these sons of the sod, poor, poor white trash, deserters . . . from the rebel army, trudged along their weary way, having more the appearance of . . . malefactors going to execution than men returning to their wives and families."

In all, 6,797 Georgia soldiers and 79 officers deserted, and in good part Brown's militiamen were little more than organized draft-evaders. In northwest Georgia, particularly in Brown's own county, the deserters and local inhabitants assumed such dangerous and rebellious proportions that General Lee himself had to rush down to suppress them. Some thousands of deserters fled from the state, only to resume marauding elsewhere.

Robert Toombs blamed it all on conscription: "We never had a desertion until we had conscription, for . . . there were thousands outside who waited to take the places of those inside. . . . Men who felt an interest in the cause stepped forward full of energy and enthusiasm. . . . Conscription and conscription alone destroyed all that feeling."

Probably more actual looting was done by Southern marauders than by Sherman's "Bummers," though he has been blamed for all the depredation. Hosts of thieves attached themselves to the flanks of his forces and fanned out to loot homes rich or poor. Everybody had to go armed. The bushwackers are everywhere, said a returning soldier.

"Fancy a ragged man," wrote Pepper, "blackened by the smoke of many a knot fire, mounted on a scrawny mule, without a saddle, with a gun, knapsack, a kitchen knife, and a plug hat, stealing his way through the pine forests far out on the flanks of a column, keen on the scent of rebels, or bacon, or silver spoons or coon, or anything valuable. He browbeat lone women and children, pried open chests or knocked furniture, tables, pianos, chairs, to pieces, tore bed clothing into three-inch strips. They searched Negro cabins, and mansions for diamonds and gold watches, with a spirit of 'pure cussedness.'" One asked for sorghum, but the jug was too heavy. So he filled his canteen, then pushed his wad of tobacco into the jug. "Why do you spoil what you don't want?" the woman asked. "Oh, some feller'll come along and taste that sorghum, think you've poisoned him; then he'll burn your damned old house." Pepper estimated that three-fifths (in value) of the personal property of the county the army passed through was looted, not by invading soldiers, but by these Georgia riffraff themselves.

In Florida most of the poor whites who could do so evaded conscription and gave information to the invaders. In the fall of 1862 the governor asked the legislature to stop speculation by Northerners who were falsely posing as loyal citizens and practicing extortion by charging outrageous prices, as well as giving information to the enemy, encouraging slaves to run away, and provoking disloyalty among the poor. Because of the draft, the land could not be tended, and many families throughout the state were in dire want.

These were people for whom the loss of a cow or two or the failure of a five-acre crop meant ruin. It meant starvation if the man of the house was taken off. On top of that, arrogant tax agents came for the ten per cent tax-in-kind and army impressment agents often seized everything people had, leaving them without a crust of bread.

Early in 1863, in Alabama and Florida, the ineffable General Pillow was given twenty special units to locate deserters, even hunting them in forests and swamps with bloodhounds. But the resisters knew every trail by pass and creek, and he was badly hampered by contradictory instructions from Richmond.

Only half a dozen in each hundred of those drafted ever showed up. By October, 1863, armed bands in the west coastal swamps were joined by swarms of deserters from other states. People in Marianna, in northwestern Jackson County, Mississippi, even threatened to raise the United States flag. Everywhere newly elected officials were either deserters or men in the army. The governor refused to permit them to be sworn in to office unless ordered to do so by the Attorney General. By 1864 conditions were still worse.

One Colonel H. D. Capers, looking for deserters, broke into the home of William Strickland, leader of the rangers of northwestern Taylor County, Florida—"The Royal Rangers"—where he found a membership list of 35 men and the constitution of the order. "We the undersigned . . . will bear true allegiance to the United States of America." They pledged to obey their elected officers, give no information, disclose nothing even to their wives and children about any proposed action, to shoot all spies, mete out death to renegades or violators of secrecy. All orders issued relative to the killing of cattle and seizure of provisions had to be cheerfully obeyed, but friends could not be abused or their property taken. They raided plantations beyond the swamps for grain and bacon, and all property was used for the common benefit. Strickland's home also yielded 2,000 rounds of ammunition, flour from the U.S. Supply Department, and other materials that proved he had regular communication with Federal gunboats in Florida waters. Colonel Capers drove out the families of all men on the list and burned all houses, including Strickland's, on both banks of the Econfina and Fenhollow Rivers.

The outlaw leader wrote defiantly that since his men had seen the burning of their homes, he could no longer control them and would no longer be responsible for whatever they might do. Officers on both sides were more wind than work. He would not fight any more for anybody, but if he and his men were allowed to stay in Taylor County, they would raise stock for the Confederates. Even if Capers had twice as many men and dogs, Strickland said his own men would never fight in the war. If they couldn't get a furlough for the deserters from Jefferson Davis, he would "remain a flea . . . and when you put your thumb on me and raise it up, I will be gone. Just set me and my men free from war."

Capers replied that all deserters had to return to their outfits, but they would be used only to tend and drive beef if they voluntarily surrendered. Few did.

Early in 1864 the armed bands captured 10,000 army blankets and 6,000 pairs of army shoes, leaving the Confederate forces without these badly needed supplies. They planned to seize the Governor of Florida himself but, forewarned, he escaped.

General F. K. Gardner, former commander of Port Hudson on the Mississippi, angrily ordered all deserters not surrendering to be shot, their homes and barns burned, their families sent into the interior. But the marauding merely grew worse. By then the armed groups were well supplied by the Federals, massed on Santa Rosa Island, where the sheriff and well-known citizens brought horses for raiders and guided them.

Presently fifty-two men of the most reliable Confederate company in West Florida deserted, indignant at the heartless treatment of the rights of citizens. So said Governor John Milton himself with a blast at the Impressment Act. They had gone home to protect their families, left helpless without cows or grain or food. Some joined the Union forces. By August a band of five hundred pro-Union men, deserters and Negroes, were raiding towards Gainesville, a large town for those times. During the entire war, of all those who deserted from Florida units, only two hundred ever returned to the army.

In Mississippi, deserters and Union sympathizers raided for food and plundered the countryside, especially northwest of the Tallahatchie River. There Confederate Captain Rison, a Peace Society member, deserted with all his men and called on all soldiers to join him, promising free quarters and brigandage.

Senator Phelan informed Davis that the loyal elements were merely a Spartan band, while the timid, the traitor and the timeserver were legion, and the state swarmed with deserters. Whole bands of them even appeared at the polls and voted. In central Jones County, the deserters set up the so-called Jones County Republic.

As early as late 1861, a Tennessee deserter held in a north Mississippi prison gave his reasons:

> The secession cause has thus far been sustained by deception and falsehood, by falsehood as the action of Congress; by false despatches as to battles . . . never fought and victories . . . never won; by false accounts as to the purpose of the President . . . ; and its progress has been marked by the most alarming and dangerous attacks upon human liberty.

The Confederate Government had been set up without proper consultation with all the states and the people and without exhausting peaceable remedies. It had opened the door to oppressive taxation without consulting the people. Its elections had been a mockery forcing sanction of its usurpations at the point of the bayonet.

When Grant took up strong positions for the formal siege of

Vicksburg in midsummer of 1863, people began to pour in, to look, to see relatives, to care for the wants of sick and wounded. Often they brought poultry. The soldiers, remarked Grant, had lived so much on chickens, ducks, and turkeys without bread, that the sight of poultry almost took away their appetites. But the intention was good, he added. The interior was full of deserters from Pemberton's Confederate army, said Grant, men determined not to fight again while the war lasted. They want to get to their homes or go North to work till the war was over. There was considerable peace feeling on all sides in Mississippi.

All Confederate offices in the state were jammed with able-bodied young men holding down jobs, and making little or no effort to enforce the laws. The army would get more conscripts, said Inspector General H. W. Walter dismally, if it closed down the conscription offices and sent the able-bodied personnel off to the front. Of 1,125 men examined for the draft at Brookhaven in southern Lincoln County, from April to October, 1864, only 218 were certified. In all Mississippi during the last five months of that year nearly all taken deserted at once, and of the 233 actually sent to the front, few ever arrived there. At the close of 1864 the number of deserters in the state, hiding out or roving about, was estimated at 7,000.

The state was being plundered by everybody with a pinch of power; by deserters with guns, by Federals, by plantation owners getting rich selling their cotton to the foe in return for luxuries, including barrels of whiskey not essential to the war effort. A planter, William Crump, Sr., controlled the local mobs of deserters for his own benefit with free whiskey.

In Texas, also, opposition became general. Many fled north. More bands of Unionists, conscripts, deserters, and others hid in the hills or roamed about lawlessly. The militia simply refused to arrest deserters. In December, 1862, a band of six hundred men from five counties, armed to resist both state and Confederate conscription, was reported in upper Austin County. General E. Kirby Smith, C.S.A., commanding the Far West, reported such a crisis in Tarrant County (Fort Worth) and other parts of the state, that it had become a question whether the Confederate forces could even control events. The deserters picketed every road and a thousand more were encamped in the woods. There were two thousand deserters fortified near the Red River. When Colonel Hobby's regiment was ordered to Galveston, so many men refused to obey that not enough were left to arrest them. Texas recruits refused to go into Louisiana even to scout. In 1863 private homes were searched for deserters. If none were found, the women and children were stripped of every bite of food. This merely made matters worse, of course.

In 1862 Davis set aside *habeas corpus* in order to give the Army a free hand to meet civil disobedience, draft evasions, and desertions, but the Texas courts, backed up by the governor, freely granted writs of *habeas corpus* to both conscripts and deserters, and the governor allowed evaders and deserters to enlist in local defense organizations, not to be sent out of the state.

Besides the terrifying food riots by soldiers in Galveston, there were fifty or sixty desertions every day. By the spring of 1865 the Confederate forces in Texas were breaking up.

Well before the end of 1864 all the states were hanging on to their volunteers and conscripts and not sending them to the Confederate army. Disintegration was well under way. The war within a war had swelled to disastrous proportions.

5. Revolt in Tennessee

East Tennessee, embracing thirty large counties, was always an embattled pro-Union area, one that never submitted to the Confederate Government. The resistance movement remained alive and fighting throughout the war. When the region was occupied by Confederate forces, many Unionists were assassinated, but, in reply, bridges were blown up, soldiers attacked and killed, and pro-Confederate citizens seized, murdered and their property destroyed. Throughout, it was an ugly *local* civil war, with terror on both sides.

Almost surrounded by high mountains, the great Cumberland range north and west separates east Tennessee from Kentucky and from the rest of the state. In the northwest, fifty miles of interlocking lakes are set like gems in the prongs of the heights. To the southeast, on the borders of North Carolina and Georgia, rise the lofty crests of the Chilhowee and Iron mountains, part of the Alleghenies. Because of its fertile Holston River Valley, its lakes and wooded hills, the region called itself the Switzerland of America.

East Tennessee was as distinct from middle and western Tennessee as from any adjoining state, even more so because it is a natural extension of southwest Virginia—one slanting corridor —the same people, soil, and climate. This area also remained militantly pro-Union throughout the war.

The area was a center of food crops and stock-raising. Horses, mules, cattle, hogs, and sheep were exported to the Atlantic states. Indian corn and wheat were staples, and rye, oats, buckwheat, potatoes (sweet and Irish), apples, peaches, pears, and

: 75 :

plums, wool, flax, and hay were produced. Butter and cheese were of superior quality. Gold had been found. The most abundant minerals were iron, copper, zinc, and lead. High-grade coal was plentiful in all the counties, and a railroad was being built from Knoxville to the coal and iron banks at the foot of the Cumberland Mountains, to connect with Kentucky and Ohio.

Only one person in twelve, as compared to one in four in the state at large, was a Negro. Nearly all the slaveholders—36,844 in a population of more than a million—lived in western Tennessee, the cotton country. Only 47 had more than 100 slaves each. Yet this handful of big plantation owners dominated the state and considered Unionists pernicious lice, a standing menace to the "peculiar institution."

Tennessee's chief markets and its main ties were really with the North, upon which it was dependent for all manufactured

Tennessee and east Tennessee. Armed resistance, sporadic elsewhere, persisted in east Tennessee throughout war.

: 76 :

and processed goods. Secession propaganda did not circulate much until the crisis was close at hand, although state historian J. G. M. Ramsay announced solemnly that "the days of the Union were numbered," that the high-toned New England spirit had degenerated into "clannish Yankeeism" and that the masses of the North were "venal, covetous, mean and selfish." He eulogized the proud cavaliers, the superiority of slaveowners, the virtue and integrity of the Huguenot, and the probity and honor of Presbyterians. But this was not the true language of frontier Tennessee, which, except in parts of the cotton area, preferred to emphasize its democracy, not its aristocracy. Many Tennesseans were sons of New England settlers, and such phrases as "nasty Puritans," and "crooked, uncouth, and immoral Yankees" did not go down well. Speaking in Knoxville in 1860, the Alabama firebrand, William Yancey, was jeered when he said: "in the North women work and white men black boots and drive carriages, while we in the South . . . more elevated . . . have Negroes to do this."

Circuit rider and editor the Reverend William G. Brownlow, in his widely read Whig newspaper, frequently sneered at the so-called Tennessee aristocrats, calling them descendants in direct line of foreigners who had been sold upon shares to pay their passage to this country; they had begun life, he said, peddling pins and needles, by spading gardens for other people or by entering other people's land and then by hook or crook securing titles.

Most Protestant ministers, except the Methodists, were against secession, while some even opposed slavery. But Reverend Harrison of the Knoxville Presbyterian Church preached that Jesus Christ was a Southerner, born on Southern soil, and so were his apostles, except Judas, who was a Northern man. He said he would sooner have a Bible printed and bound in hell than north of the Mason and Dixon line. Unfortunately nearly all Bibles used in the South came from the North. Many fellow ministers were Confederate.

Brownlow was bitter about it:

Ascending the pulpit on the Lord's day, under a pretense of "feeding the sheep," those reverend traitors to God and their country deliver inflammatory stump speeches, excite the worst passions of a people not extravagantly given to prayer, and thus more effectually serve the cause of the devil than [do] the ultra-Abolition preachers of the North. . . . The South is now full of these reverend traitors . . . preachers don't make any *better* traitors than the most abandoned sinners. . . . Counterfeiting money or forging checks . . . are not less wicked acts because perpetrated by a preacher than . . . if perpetrated by an infamous gambler.

When war hysteria sweeps over a whole people, the human mass becomes a dangerous frightening torrent, but Brownlow never faltered, either in jail or out, in his Union loyalty. "Hoist your miserable cabbage leaf of a Palmetto flag," he cried when South Carolina seceded, "but depend upon it, men and brethern, you will be dashed to pieces on the rocks." He warned Governor Isham G. Harris of Tennessee, who was moving heaven and earth to destroy his state's resistance to secession, that he would take up a bayonet and resist. The Confederates would have to walk over his dead body and the dead bodies of every man in east Tennessee.

The press had been largely pro-Union, but it also swung South. The Whig Nashville *Banner* had denounced the vile, deep-laid plot to destroy the citizens' liberties, to "chloroform them with sectional prejudices." The Memphis *Inquirer* called secession a madman's remedy. Both papers soon jumped into the Confederate net.

"Secession has assumed an *epidemic* fear in most . . . southern states," wrote Brownlow. "It is nothing to know that a particular man was a Union man, last night, how is he this morning . . . ? Men rise up and dress as Union men, and turn Secessionist before breakfast is over. . . . The disease is contagious, . . . a clever man will contract it by drinking mean whisky out of the same tumbler with one addicted with it."

Andrew Johnson, a strong pro-Union advocate, was burned in

effigy by proslavery bigots and on a speaking tour was hissed and hooted all along the route. Brownlow reprinted his exposé of a scheme by the local postmaster, a Congressman, and local bankers to defraud a Northern capitalist and Johnson's character by forging letters asking for money to buy arms. Governor Harris, though knowing the letters were forged, gave them to the press. Senator Wigfall of Texas, a noted duellist and Secessionist, busily publicized the canard. He was to become an inveterate enemy of Jefferson Davis in the Confederacy.

For January 7, 1861, the governor called a special legislative session. He recited all the imaginary Northern abuses against the South, but got little response and could not get a mandate to call a convention to vindicate the sovereignty of the state. He did manage to push through a call for a plebiscite on whether to convene such a convention and to elect representatives for it should the vote be affirmative.

In east Tennessee only pro-Union candidates emerged. Mountain men attended rallies with guns in hand and reacted violently against secession talk. The convention call was swamped there, and the state at large was 4 to 1 against it. Only four counties in all Tennessee gave a majority to Secessionist candidates. Former Governor William B. Campbell warned, however, that Harris planned to use troops and vigilantes to browbeat the people into secession.

Encouraged by the vote, Brownlow ran in the August elections as an independent for the governorship. His eyes, he told the voters, had not been blinded by telescopes made of cotton stalks. The Secession leaders would "go down to their graves without any halo of glory surrounding their brows, while on their heads would be gathered the hissing curses of all generations, terrible as the fork-tongued snakes of Medusa. Their ghosts will stand on the highest and blackest eminence of infamy. . . . Their monument will be the human bones upon foundations slippery with human blood." But he was laid low by bronchitis and had to withdraw. By then Tennessee had already seceded.

Lincoln's call for volunteers gave new arguments to the local

Confederates. Harris cried that he wanted not one man to attack the South, but promised 50,000 for the Confederacy. He convened a second special legislative session. A prominent Secessionist promised cold steel and bullets, passions rose, and anti-Secessionists began crawling into the cocoon of neutrality. The landslide of fanaticism had set in.

The most pitiful turncoat was the ex-Know-Nothing, Constitutional Union candidate for the Presidency, John Bell. Horace Greeley called him weak and culpable for being beguiled into the crime of dividing and destroying the country. James G. Blaine, a self-seeker himself, said that Bell, his party and half a million Southern Whigs could have paralyzed the secession movement. Brownlow, a lifelong supporter of Bell, broke with him publicly, tears in his eyes.

In thundering tones, Harris called on the legislature for immediate separation. He would strip himself naked rather than see his neighbors and their children in bondage to the vandal Lincoln government. He promptly forced through an ordinance to be submitted to the voters. Outrageous tyranny, Brownlow's *Whig* and other papers called it. The legislators, however, after listening to an eloquent Davis emissary, voted to put the militia under Confederate command and invited the Confederate government to make Nashville its permanent capital.

Brownlow urged the people to vote against the ordinance or Tennessee would be swallowed up by a military despotism more odious than any in Europe. But the rowdies were already at work, lawlessly night-riding, and it became dangerous even in east Tennessee to vote against secession. Men were killed, their homes burned, while Unionist papers were suppressed or wrecked. "We are in the midst of terror," Brownlow wrote three weeks before the election. "Whether my humble voice is hushed in death, or my press is muzzled, I beg you . . . all . . . to credit no Secessionist falsehood which may represent me as having changed."

Only in parts of east Tennessee was any sort of pro-Union campaign carried on. Out-of-state soldiers were rushed in, quartered in new Confederate camps, and allowed to vote, 6,241 of them. Five thousand citizens, it was alleged, were deterred from voting by threats of violence. In spite of this the vote against secession was 33,000 to 18,300, though in the state as a whole the ordinance was adopted by a vote of more than 2 to 1. The Unionists insisted that the state had been taken out of the Union by fraud and villainy, and that the Union men would have the state back in the fold soon or die in the ditch.

A few prominent Unionists were elected to Congress and instead of going to Richmond took their seats in Washington. One was arrested en route and escaped by taking an oath of allegiance to the Confederacy. Another was lured back by the false report that his wife was dying, but he escaped again by the Underground Railroad.

The east Tennessee Unionists, in an armed convention in Greenville, denounced the violent elections as fraudulent, reaffirmed their national allegiance and petitioned the legislature to permit east Tennessee to become an independent state.

Instead, hundreds of Unionists were arrested and those who would not take the Confederate oath and pay court costs were sent to concentration camps. The Reverend William Duggan, a poor man with six small children, was charged with having prayed for the Union and, though aged, weighing 280 pounds, and still recovering from an attack of fever, was driven on foot without food and water for seven miles until he collapsed. He was prodded back to his feet with bayonets.

Not until February 16, 1862, did Northern forces push into the western part of the state. The panic-stricken legislators looted the state bank, burned the archives, destroyed or stole public property, and ignominiously fled with Harris to the Confederate army. General Grant declared martial law, and Lincoln named Andrew Johnson as the war, or military, governor. He offered amnesty to all who would swear allegiance, but plots were made to kill him; guerrilla bands tried to capture his train; General Bragg cooked up a scheme to kidnap him. Andrew Johnson arrested seven vociferous Secessionists, six of them ministers, shut down a pro-Davis daily paper and Baptist and Methodist publishing houses. The knife was cutting the other way now—with equal intolerance. Lincoln tried to placate the state, and other border states, by offering to pay for all slaves, but the owners merely moved their blacks farther south. A judge's election was won by a Confederate sympathizer, and Johnson began feuding with the Union military authorities. The regular December elections could not be held, since Confederate cavalry raids and vigilantes drove out the Unionist candidates.

It was two years more before Federal troops took over east Tennessee. During those years terrible things happened. The seven thousand Confederate troops, at first under General E. Kirby Smith, were able to rule only by terror. Attempts to call up the local militia failed. Unionists fled in bands of twenty to a hundred men through the interminable dense laurel thickets and across the Cumberland Mountains to Kentucky. As early as May, 1862, there were enough in Kentucky to form the South Tennessee Regiment (U.S.), men impatient to get back to their families and recover their homes.

The Confederate position was far from impregnable, said Brownlow. The occupying forces were undisciplined recruits, poorly armed with squirrel guns and shotguns taken from Union men. Their small cannon were not equal in number or calibre with those of the Federal army. Many would never fight against the Stars and Stripes, and the people were merely waiting for the appearance of Northern troops to range themselves under their banner.

Morale was bad, and Brownlow's opinion was shared by many Confederate officers. One major reported, "The Union feeling of this county is exceedingly bitter, and all want . . . to induce a general uprising. . . . They have a great many arms, and are actually manufacturing Union flags to receive the refugee Tennesseans when they return."

Vengeance on both sides was the order of the day. Family feuds became deadly. Robbery and murder were rampant. Bands of scoundrels scoured the area, calling old farmers to their doors and shooting them down in cold blood. It was a war at every man's door, neighbor against neighbor. No one's property or life was safe.

The Memphis *Appeal*, on November 16, 1861, contained the following advertisement by two Confederate officers:

Bloodhounds Wanted. We, the undersigned, will pay five dollars per pair for fifty pairs of well-bred hounds, and fifty dollars for one pair of thoroughbred bloodhounds that will take the track of man. The purpose . . . to chase the infernal cowardly Lincoln bushwackers of East Tennessee and Kentucky. . . .

In April, 1862, a commentator wrote, "The work of murder, arrests and imprisonments goes evenly in east Tennessee. They are shooting Union men down in the streets, and killed, in one instance, fifty or sixty after they surrendered. They marched between three and four hundred loyal citizens, some . . . barefooted and their feet bleeding, to the depot, and shipped them to Georgia to work upon their forts." Denied water, they had to lift it by cupping their hands, out of mud puddles in the streets.

N. G. Taylor, a Conservative Congressman, memorialized the United States Congress about these conditions.

Their [the Unionists] arms and ammunition were seized before they could organize by the rebel soldiers; and though the [Washington] government . . . did not protect them, yet their hearts clung to the government, and they payed for the Union. Five thousand of their men have seen the inside walls of rebel prisons, and hundreds of them, covered with filth, devoured by vermin, famished with hunger, have died martyrs for their country. . . . Their property has been seized, confiscated; their houses pillaged . . . their substance wasted; their fences burned; their fields laid waste; their farms destroyed by friends as well as foes. The rebels robbed them; the Federals devoured them, for they had short supplies; and our women broke their last biscuit and gave them the biggest half, out of the mouths of hungry children. They gave up the last horse, mule, cow, sheep, hog, everything they had to the soldiers that needed them, because they were Union soldiers, or were plundered out of them by the enemy. Their young men had been hunted like wild beasts, by soldiers, by Indians, sometimes by bloodhounds, and when caught, tied two-and-two by long ropes and driven before cavalry—thin-clad, barefooted, others shot down in their homes . . . or the fields, or in the forests; others still have been hung up by the neck to the limbs of trees, without judge or jury. I have heard of no single neighborhood within the bounds of East Tennessee whose green sod did not drink the blood of citizens murdered.

"The real traitors . . ." Brownlow kept on, undaunted, "are Yancey, Rhett, Toombs, Pryor, Davis, Keitte, Iverson, Wise, Mason, Wigfall and Breckinridge. . . . They have misled and deceived the Southern people to the ruin of the country. And when the reaction takes place—as it surely will—popular vengeance will seek them out for punishment." If the war continued three to five years, he stated, they would all be refugees in foreign countries. He paid especial attention to grafting and thievery, quoting papers from all over the South. Swindling had outstripped any thieving ever heard of in the history of war. Robbers, disguised as merchants, were preying on helpless women while their men were at the front. Printed money had been stolen from the Treasury Building itself. Horse thieves sold, stole and resold worthless horses to the army at high prices. "Whiskey preaching chaplains should quote the Bible that 'nor thieves nor covetous drunkards nor revilers nor extortionists shall inherit the kingdom of God' "—this from the Richmond *Enquirer*.

The east Tennessee situation deteriorated steadily for the Confederacy as more and more citizens took up arms. One officer reported a band in Roane County, west of Knoxville, with 175 men. Six bridge-burners were caught and hung, two of them on an oak limb close to the railroad tracks so passengers could curse them, hit them with canes, and spit on their bodies. But more bridges were burned. Major-General Felix Zollicoffer, C.S.A., ordered all inhabitants disarmed, but had to fall back to Cumberland Ford, and his regular troops were promptly attacked and many wounded. By the end of 1862, a pro-Unionist named Clift had 1,500 armed men in Bradley County and was being joined by other troops. "One band of 78 men equipped with knapsacks and guns. Nine hundred moved out in squads to organize operations against Lowden bridge or else to join Unionists forces from Kentucky . . . , have some wagons and are partly armed. . . . Formidable."

On November 12, the commanders at Charleston and Chattanooga telegraphed that a certain Jeff Mathias was within twelve miles with a hundred men and they were encamped near Smith's crossroads. Help was needed immediately to disperse them.

Up until the day of secession, Brownlow had kept a small United States flag flying, and all through 1861 and early 1862 he published innumerable letters he received, all threatening to tar, feather, or hang him. "You will certainly be hung, as all dogs should be, until you are 'dead, dead, dead,' " wrote William Yancey. Just before the 1861 elections he was sent a package containing pus-soaked bandages from a smallpox patient.

Every day gangs of civilians or soldiers came to Brownlow's residence, pointing guns and knives at the windows and threatening his life. They were instigated by the temporary commander of Knoxville, the Reverend (Colonel) W. B. Wood, an Alabaman, who preached in the Methodist church on Sunday. But in mid-1861, regiments fresh from the cotton states, whom Brownlow called the worst riff-raff of New Orleans, Mobile, and Texas, after visiting the whiskey shops, swarmed about his printing office and home, howling like wolves, swearing and threatening to hang him and kill his wife and three children. Mobs kept returning all summer and fall.

The military seized his press in November, and he was indicted on sundry charges. In his last issue he wrote: "I have committed no offense . . . advocated no rebellion against the Confederacy . . . [but had refused] to make war on the government of the United States. . . . President Davis had said he could not live in a country that did not tolerate freedom of the press." The object of his "arrest and contemplated imprisonment," Brownlow continued, "is to dry up, break down, silence and destroy the last and only Union paper left in the eleven seceded states. I shall feel proud of my confinement. I shall go to jail—as John Rodgers went to the stake—for my principles. . . . I shall go because . . . of . . . the most wicked, cruel, unnatural and uncalled-for war ever recorded in history."

After the paper was seized, mob threats were directed against his home, and to relieve the danger for his family, he rode to adjacent counties to collect money due for past advertising. While he was at Blount the railroad bridges were burned. He was blamed as the instigator and messengers brought word to him at Sevierville where he was preaching that Colonel Wood had sent out cavalry with orders to shoot him on sight.

With a number of legislators, preachers, and planters, he fled into the Great Smoky Mountains on the North Carolina border. Friends brought them food and they killed a bear, which provided meat. They were now high up on the east fork of Little River, and a large force would have been required to take them.

Tiring of moving hither and yon, he and several companions rode down to Unionist friends six miles from Knoxville. From there he wrote Confederate General W. H. Carroll, then in charge of the city, telling how he had been driven from his home by threats but had no knowledge of the bridge burning. He was willing to appear and be tried, but did not wish to be turned over to any infuriated group of armed men.

Carroll offered him guarantees of personal safety with civil hearings. But the general was a notorious drunkard and lived in the house of a man (one of three) Brownlow had previously exposed as a bank swindler. The other two now had charge of the district attorney's office and the local court. One, Brownlow wrote, had already tried to have him murdered by drunken troops. Along with a businessman and a 77-year-old preacher, Brownlow forwarded a notarized oath of innocence. He reasserted his loyalty to the United States, but merely wished to be left alone to enjoy his private opinions.

Word came from the Attorney General in Richmond that if Brownlow would give himself up within twenty-four hours, he would be provided with a passport to go to Kentucky. At once he presented himself at the headquarters of General Crittenden. The general offered him a cavalry escort to the Federal lines to leave December 7, two days later. But the parson was arrested by District Attorney J. C. Ramsey on a charge of treason based on his writings before secession.

Brownlow protested to Crittenden, but the latter said the safe conduct gave him no protection against civil investigations.[1]

Brownlow wrote Secretary Benjamin, reminding him of the safe conduct pledge and asking how a third-rate, dirty, drunken little county-clerk lawyer could take him out of the hands of General Crittenden and cast him into prison. "I am anxious to learn which is your high authority. Just give me my passports, and I will do for your Confederacy more than the devil has ever done—I will quit the country."

In jail, so crowded some had to stand to let others sleep, Brownlow found about 150 pro-Union men, old and young, of all professions and colors. Not a bed, bench, stool, table or any furniture whatever existed. The food was unfit for a dog—scraps and leavings from a dirty hotel kept by the jailer. Drinking water was drawn in a filthy wooden bucket from a hogshead in which the guards washed their hands and faces. He was told, "By God, Sir, we will have you know that where a Jeff Davis man washes his face and hands is good enough for any damned Lincolnite to drink."

Brownlow told his fearful fellow prisoners that they should take glory in their imprisonment, that the Federal government would crush the wicked rebellion and liberate them all. If they were brutally shot, they would die in a good cause. "I regard this as the proudest day of my life."

---

[1] Later on, according to Brownlow, Ramsay assembled a few volunteers, got his fingers on army funds, and was drummed out of Zollicoffer's camp with his hands tied behind his back and a placard labeled THIEF on his chest. Presently another of the bank swindlers who had helped put Brownlow behind bars was thrust into jail by five fellow officers for having embezzled $40,000 of army funds.

The following day, forty prisoners were taken off to the state prison in Tuscaloosa, and twenty-one new ones came in. They brought tales of woe about the maltreatment of Union men and their families by drunken and debauched cavalry. The rebels were stealing everything, entering houses, breaking open drawers and chests, and vigilantes were prowling the countryside like wolves. Mobs, armed to the teeth, were shooting people down in home and field. A Unionist Methodist preacher was shot down in his own garden.

The next day an alleged bridge-burner, C. A. Ham, was brought in, tried at once by a drumhead court-martial, then was taken off in a cart sitting on his own coffin and hung. He left a wife and small children.

But on December 18, sixty prisoners were released after long imprisonment, being told there was nothing against them and that their arrest had been a mistake. However, an old man and his son were taken out and hung. The son was hung first so the father would have to watch it. Brownlow added in his diary, "A pro-Union man was brought in from Campbell County to-day. The wife was killed and six small children left behind."

General Carroll, more drunk than usual, visited Brownlow and offered to free him if he would take an oath of allegiance. Brownlow told him he preferred to lie there and die before doing so, and called the Confederacy a big Southern mob, not a government.

He became desperately ill with bronchitis. The doctor had to put a silken cord down his windpipe to enable him to breathe. General Carroll offered to have him taken to a hospital. Brownlow said he wanted no passport to be poisoned within twenty-four hours.

> This was a terrible night! The sentinels all drunk—howling like wolves—rushing to our windows with the ferocity of Sepoys of India and daring the prisoners to show their heads—cocking their guns and firing off three of them into the jail, and pretending it was accidental. Merciful God! How long are we to be treated in this fashion?

Near Christmas the troops went on a spree, and twenty-five of *them* were thrust into the jail. They yelled all night like savages, some cursing Lincoln, others cursing Davis. "Write this at midnight." Five days later, twelve more drunk soldiers were thrust into their tight cell. Three prisoners were lying on the floor, too sick to move. By New Year, Brownlow himself was so desperately ill that the doctor got him transferred to his home under guard. He had to stay in bed for two months with no visitors allowed.

The Secretary of War brought pressure on the local court to cancel the charges against him on the grounds that because of previous promises, the honor of the Confederacy was at stake. The local *Register* reported that as soon as he could travel, he would be sent to the "Hessian" lines. On January 28, a Colonel Leadbetter informed him arrogantly he had to get out at once, and two days later a drunken captain read him an order. He was to be taken to the hospital to prevent him from plotting treason.

His doctor had this rescinded, but a double guard was placed about his home. Except for seeing his family, he was held incommunicado. Two sentinels stood at each of the ever open doors of his room day and night, and the shouting and swearing of the others made sleep impossible. They congregated in his office, library, and back yard, playing cards, breaking furniture, ruining the carpets, and mutilating his books. His coal and wood and food were used up, and none of the family was permitted to go to market. One soldier came down with measles, and only Brownlow's wife and two Negroes escaped infection. To both serve the troops meals and care for the sick became almost impossible.

On February 24 he was ordered taken to Richmond. He protested that this was bad faith, and on March 2, Secretary Benjamin ordered him taken out as soon as possible through the Cumberland Gap or any other safe route and turned over to the Federals under a flag of truce. Unable to travel on horseback, he asked to be shipped out by way of Memphis.

On the train, drunken troops tried to lynch him, but his five-man guard held them off. In Wartrace, General A. Sidney Johnston ordered him taken home again or released. Either order meant death. He would be mobbed in Wartrace, where Morgan's "mob of cavalry" (as he put it) had vowed to kill him, and he could not physically stand the trip back.

His escort hurried him on to Decatur, where General Crittenden gave new orders that he be taken out under a flag of truce. But General Hardee refused to honor the orders. For three days, Brownlow and the five guards shared a filthy room that cost Brownlow sixty dollars. Not until March 15 were they allowed to proceed along the turnpike to Nashville, then held by the Federals.

He was warmly received and taken at once to talk with the commanding officer.

On April 21, Colonel Churchwell ordered Brownlow's wife Eliza and the three children to leave the Confederacy within thirty-six hours. She had to abandon everything.

His story had preceded him and, despite his bronchitis, he spoke briefly to large audiences.

> They're nearly out of soap down South. They lack guns, clothing, boots and shoes. . . . They are out of hats, too. In Knoxville, there is not a bolt of bleached domestic or calico to be had, not a spool of Coates thread; and though cotton is king, we have never made a spool of thread south of the Mason and Dixon line. Sewing needles and pins are not to be had. . . . It has been remarked on the streets of Knoxville that no such thing as a fine-toothed comb was to be had, and all the little secession heads were full of squatter sovereigns [lice] hunting for their rights in the territories.

His health and confidence improved steadily, and his trip to the northeast became a triumphal tour.

His loss of his home, newspaper, and all his property was recovered by his published memoirs, which brought him sixty thousand dollars. As soon as the war was over, he returned to Tennessee, started a newspaper, and served as Reconstruction governor. Despite his earlier support of slavery, he gave the Negroes full citizenship, and when violence was used to keep them from voting, he provided them with guns to enforce their rights. He helped them in every way until the Ku Klux Klan, headed by General Forrest, returned the old regime to power by night-riding, murder, and terror.

6. Mississippi at Bay

Governor John Jones Pettus, a long-standing Secessionist, called on Mississippi to "go down into Egypt as long as Herod rules over Judea," and six weeks later, on January 9, 1861, the special convention at Jackson voted to take the state out of the Union.

The Democratic Party had split badly over secession as early as 1851, then to regain unity, had for some years clawed dirt over the issue. But the fire eaters were soon active again, though not until John Brown's raid did they manage to arouse widespread fear. Vigilante violence thereafter terrorized whole counties. Newly elected Abraham Lincoln became a monster, used to frighten babies in the cradle, and no free elections could be held that December, 1861. There were only contests of armed violence, preceded by wholesale killings of anti-Secessionists, antislavery men, and Union supporters, many taken from their homes and strung up on convenient limbs by strong hemp.

It is likely that Mississippi would have seceded in any case, yet it *was* badly divided, and without strong-arm tactics it might have revealed these differences to the world. In any case it is always difficult for peace-loving people to resist an organized war party or to withstand ever mounting hysteria and mass emotions that sweep away men's reason. Prewar intimidation and violence are usually a necessary prelude to armed action.

The ruling Mississippi triumvirate was said to be the large slaveowning plantation holder, the moneylender, and the (lawyer) politician. By no means did all the big slaveowners, mostly Whigs, favor secession and war; they were content with their

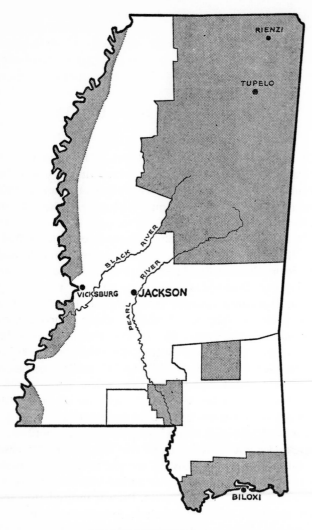

MISSISSIPPI

Mississippi. Chief areas of armed resistance. By 1862 in northern counties, along the Mississippi and the Gulf, and around upper reaches of main rivers. Later, nearly all counties.

existing power and privileges, which were in no way seriously menaced. On the other hand, nearly all the poor people in the extensive pine woods areas were jealous of their independence and wanted to be left alone, however miserable their existence. If not particularly pro-Union, they were antiwar, often militantly so all along the Black and Pearl Rivers in central and south Mississippi, the more so as the country grew hilly or mountainous. Yet even in Hinds County itself, the location of Jackson, the state capital, the small farmers—and they made up the bulk of the population, except for Negroes—were almost unanimously pro-Union. So were the people of most of the northern counties. Jones County in south central Mississippi was a heroic outpost of Federal zeal. The scrubby Gulf counties, with the worst soil in the state, largely dependent upon sporadic lumbering and completely dependent on food imported from New Orleans and Mobile, were bitterly opposed to secession and in due time became the haunt of free-wheeling bands of deserters from all over the state and the Confederacy at large. All the Mississippi River counties had large contingents of Union sympathizers.

Most of the large slaveowners favored secession or soon came to do so, though the more aggressive backers were the smaller and more ambitious planters with fewer slaves. Their attitude was echoed by a large share of the politicians, lawyers, preachers, merchants, and artisans fearing the competition of free Negroes, and many poor and illiterate folk, particularly of the cotton plains country. These were wont, even if barefoot, to use the expression "our slaves." Brownlow of Tennessee often told how many near paupers said they were fighting because the North had refused to permit "our slaves" to be introduced into the territories.

The convention was assembled in Jackson on January 7, 1861, under galleries filled with cheering, jeering Secessionists. In spite of the terrorism before and during the polling, a third or more of the delegates were Union men calling themselves Cooperationists, calling for an accommodation with the North, asking for at least postponement of secession and asking finally that it not take effect until most of the other Southern states had taken a similar step. How many the opposition would have numbered had the campaign and the voting been free of violence, no one knows. Reverend John Aughey related how the anti-Secession men had been terrorized in an adjacent county, and in Choctaw County, which he believed to be pro-Union, his was the one and only vote cast for a Union candidate, and this in the face of threats and menacing dark faces.

At the convention the members reviewed a military parade marching behind a fifteen-star Secession flag, and they were presented with a Bonny Blue Flag by the patriotic Jackson ladies. The recalcitrant Whigs, Unionists, Cooperationists and Pacifists, led chiefly by James L. Alcorn, were overwhelmed after a few skirmishes, and the fatal vote of separation from the Union was taken on January 9. Most of those in opposition jumped on the bandwagon, even Alcorn. Judge A. M. Clayton delivered the key speech. He began by declaring his belief in the institution of slavery—the greatest material interest on earth. Slave labor alone was able to toil in subtropical climates, and slave products provided the largest share of world commerce. A blow at slavery was a blow against commerce and civilization.

But in spite of the patriotic feeling aroused, and all the bands and flags and marching, Mississippi was still a state badly divided. It had to win a war at home while facing Northern armies, and, of course, neither war was won. Violence and terrorism grew worse as soon as secession became an actuality. The Federal courts disappeared and civil and criminal actions were dropped, many of the defendants freed of any charges. The state courts were demoralized and either ceased to sit or simply dismissed many cases. Thus the carrying out of justice became almost exclusively the function of vigilantes and the Confederate army, with or without trial. Often this lawlessness represented petty and personal grudges of long duration. Any attitude against slavery, even a chance remark of decades previous, was enough to bring prison or even the hangman's noose to many.

Many preachers had been more liberal than their communities, and had sought over the years to ameliorate the condition of the slaves, to provide them with better health and living conditions, and often had taught them to read and write in spite of the laws against such instruction. Quite a few had even been opposed to slavery, particularly the Presbyterians and, of course, the Quakers, of whom there were not many in Mississippi. But most became pro-war overnight, merely shifting their prayers to bless Davis and the Confederacy rather than the traditional blessing of the President and the Federal Government.

Quite a number, again mostly Presbyterians, stuck by their guns. Some of them were threatened, attacked, jailed or killed. If they could not be easily removed from their pulpits, as in the case of the Reverend James A. Lyon whose congregation stuck by him loyally throughout, members of their families were persecuted. Lyon's son Theodoric, though holding an army commission, was put on trial for his opinions, in a courtroom filled with drunken loudmouths who drowned out the defense lawyer with abuse. He was subsequently cashiered, conscripted, and sent to Virginia.

A vivid picture of the post-secession terror and of anti-Confederate conspiracy is given by Reverend Aughey. The account is to be found in Volume 17 (p. 207 et seq.) of the 130 volumes of *War Records,* and is told in his later books *Tupelo* and *The Fighting Parson.* He described a clandestine meeting, called together by a flaming beacon on a mountaintop, over which he presided.

> Dark hills frowned on every side; waters of a crystal spring bubbled up and in mournful cadence glided down the glen; the midnight moon gazed wistfully down from the zenith; fitful clouds and the overhanging branches of the lofty trees, stately monarchs of the woods, obscured her light. . . . Quietly approaching from all possible points human forms appeared, gliding noiselessly into the narrow area around the spring.

Sixty-five men and twenty-nine women were present.

Suddenly the little group was surprised by Confederates, led by a Major Ham who called upon them to surrender within ten minutes. "Had we surrendered not one of us would have been left alive." A storm burst, lightning flashed, thunder rolled, the rain fell in torrents. During the fighting, the women cowered about the spring except for two girls who, from behind trees, returned the fire with Navy revolvers. During the melee, in which one Unionist was killed, another wounded, and four Confederates killed, Aughey, after emptying his revolver, felled an attacker and was himself knocked down by a blow on the head. But the assailants were sent flying off in panic. Aughey himself woke up in a forest cabin, attended by the woman of the house and guarded by two Unionists with a prisoner trussed up, whom they killed in spite of Aughey's attempts to save him.

Aughey received his fourth draft notice, along with a hundred neighbors: "PARSON JOHN H. AWAY. You haven't tended nun of our musters as konscrip. Now you is hereby summenzed to attend a kort marshal at Jim Mocks, June the first." Aughey argued that they should go in a band with guns, but cavalry from Corinth was being sent, and it was decided that all should try to reach the Federal armies, then besieging Corinth.

Aughey reached Rienzi just in time to see Northern cavalry scouring the countryside, dense with the smoke of burning cotton, after fleeing Confederates. Aughey ventured back through the lines to his father-in-law's where he remained with his wife and child.

Conditions were terrible, and people were starving. Flour was $30 (U.S.) a barrel, bacon 40 cents a pound, coffee a dollar, and salt a dollar but hardly obtainable. Aughey began buying up cotton and smuggling it north, using the money gained to purchase provisions. Also, he guided Union spies to reconnoiter. They brought back Federal soldiers who killed the guards and burned a bridge at Norman.

Aughey was arrested by the Confederates and charged with spying and sedition. Unflinchingly, he reaffirmed his Unionism and his loyalty to Mississippi, where he had preached for eleven years. He had a handsome, long-jawed face, a rolled-back mane of hair and a piercing implacable gaze from under level eyebrows. He was passed from officer to officer, each growing more furious at his forthright answers. He told General Thomas Jordan, Beauregard's chief of staff, that Mississippi was still part of the Union and that the Act of Secession was unconstitutional. All Unionists, the general retorted, had been given a chance to leave the Confederacy.

"My friends who accepted Jeff Davis's permission to leave are either dead or languishing in prison. But just give me a pass to go North and I will go instanter."

"The first pass you will get will be a free ticket to hell."

"Thanks for your kind offer. . . . I was not aware before that you were the devil's ticket agent."

"Did you oppose secession?"

"I did, but now I favor it."

(Aughey meant that once its people had become convinced of their folly, they should secede from the Confederacy and resume allegiance to the Union.)

Jordan said he should be sent to hell from the lowest lateral limb of the nearest tree. He was taken before three generals, including hard-boiled General Bragg, who angrily shouted that he deserved immediate execution.

Held in Tupelo jail, he found friends and received food for the first time that day—cornbread and meat. "The meat," he was told sardonically, "makes up in strength and odor what it lacks in quality, and the parasites will impart a freshness to it." He could not sleep because of the filth and the lice, which he called "graybacks," and in the morning he could not get up because his coat was glued fast by molasses.

Many prisoners wore heavy fetters and some were chained to bolts in the floor. Nearly every day prisoners were marched out to be shot or hung. Two conscripts who had refused to serve were hung up by their thumbs. Before they were shot, Aughey baptized them with what little water was at hand. Both refused food. "We go to eat bread in the kingdom of God." As the squad marched them off, a half-dozen captive Negroes in a corner sang spirituals about the home beyond the Jordan.

"We were a motley assemblage," Aughey wrote. "All the southern states and every prominent religious denomination had representatives among us. The youth in his nonage, and the gray-haired . . . man were there. The learned . . . and the illiterate, the superior and the subordinate. . . . The descendants of Shem, Ham and Joseph were there on the same common level; in our prison were Africa's dark-browed sons, the descendants of Pocahontas, and the pure Caucasian. Death is said to be the great leveler; the dungeon at Tupelo was a great leveler. A fellow-feeling made us wondrous kind; none ate his morsel alone, and a deep and abiding sympathy for each other's woes pervaded every bosom."

A prisoner about to be shot, who had a wife and seven children, had tried to escape and managed to kill six bloodhounds with a pecan-wood club, before being wounded by cavalry and brought back. He knelt with Aughey praying for a long time. At dark he was allowed to fetch water, a bucket in each hand. He dashed the water into the faces of his two guards and jumped into the bushes.

To escape the bloodhounds, he leaped on the back of a cow. Later, lying in a ditch, he heard the hounds baying, coming closer. He caught up with another fugitive, whose house had been attacked by vigilantes, and whose daughter had been killed, while he himself was wounded. Together the two outlaws raced toward Corinth. About to be overtaken, they luckily ran into Federal cavalry, who prepared an ambush and shot and killed outright sixteen rebels picking off the rest when they tried to mount their horses. The bodies of the Confederates and the hounds were left in the bushes to be devoured by wild hogs. Both men later reached Corinth and enlisted.

An aged gentleman was shoved into Tupelo prison, one Professor Lorimer Vickeroy Yarborough of Virginia, lately of New Orleans. He and his son had been taken off the river boat and held at Vicksburg for several months. Escaping, they were rearrested by vigilantes and fed cornbread and water for six weeks. Oscar, the son, took the oath of allegiance and enlisted. At the first opportunity he deserted and later became a Union officer.

The father was unconscious with malaria for weeks. He feigned madness and was examined by General Beauregard and two alienists. General Beauregard opened the questioning.

"*What is your name?*"

"My name, capting, air old Pilgarlie. . . . It means old Baldhead. You see, capting, I ain't got no hair on the top of my head. I was born so, and when some growed on, a nigger girl applied some suma[c] on my crown, and I hain't had no hair since. . . ."

"*Where do you live?*"

"I live in a cabin with a stick chimley in Arkansas."

"*Does your chimney draw well?*"

"Yes, capting, it draws the 'tention of every fool that passes on the trail."

"*Are you a married man?*"

"Not now I aint, but . . . I have the refusal of more 'n half a dozen widders. . . ."

"*Pilgarlie, what's your opinion about this war?*"

The professor began roaring at the top of his voice,

> Spread all her canvas to the breeze,
> Set every threadbare sail. . . .

The alienists felt his pulse and inserted a thermometer in his mouth. He crunched it with his teeth and roared out

> Prudent on the council train,
> Dauntless on the battle plain.

Though one alienist thought him to be on the verge of incurable insanity, when he refused to stop singing, he was gagged and bound and thrust into Tupelo prison.

General Bragg ordered him executed on July 11. The professor refused to be blindfolded. When his supposed death struggles ceased, two conscripts, saying they were relatives, took him to a Unionist home near Tupelo. Amazingly he was not dead. His left arm had been smashed and another bullet had glanced from his ribs, while a third had passed through his clothing. With the help of neighbors, his host amputated his arm. He rallied and was passed from one Union neighbor to another toward the Federal lines at La Grange, Tennessee.

The last part of the way, pilots guided him and eight others. They were sighted by Rebel cavalry. The guides quickly tied the hands of two men behind their backs and told the cavalry captain they were taking them to headquarters.

"Good," replied Captain Prender, C.S.A., and boasted he had just shot ten "Tory" devils. "I'll go over to camp with you." He left his second in command to lead his men.

En route the pilots suggested hanging the two men then and there. They held a trial in a copse of dwarf tamaracks; the two men confessed to treason and were bound to two saplings. The pilots asked to do the shooting. "Make ready, take aim, fire," shouted the captain. The pilots shot him instead. As he fell, he yelled, "Damn the traiters!" and, without another word, "his spirit left his clay tenement."

The group raced on toward Union lines, where Yarborough rejoined his son, who by this time was a Union captain.

Meanwhile, after receiving a smuggled note signed "Charlotte Corday, my nom de guerre," from friends living two miles from Tupelo, Aughey decided to try to escape with a certain Richard Malone, whose hard eye and intelligent face impressed him. Malone had a sketch map of the route they should follow to get through the vast army encampment.

Following a Fourth of July farewell celebration, featured by a crudely made flag, and a talk by Aughey about the patriot forefathers and a warning that "a dishonored grave and a hell of torment" would be the final fate of every traitor, they sang "My Country, 'Tis of Thee" and "Rally Round the Flag, Boys." Exactly at midnight, Aughey and Malone slid under a pried-up floor plank and wriggled underneath the building toward the south enclosure where there were few guards.

The sky was covered with murky clouds; they could scarcely see. They separated. A guard, hearing a noise, peered into the enclosure. Aughey lay absolutely still, and the sentinel hurried into the prison to check. The minister crawled past other sentinels into a cornfield. There, Malone did not respond to pre-arranged signals. Hounds and cavalry would soon be hunting for them, so Aughey went on through the big camp. Sentinels were everywhere. As dawn brightened, he crawled into a dense thicket in a tupelo grove and tried to snatch some sleep. But the camp noises kept him awake, and all day soldiers passed and repassed on a trail only eight feet away. He was within thirty yards of a swimming pool in Old Town Creek.

A cannon boomed. A soldier said it was to celebrate the Bull Run victory over McClellan in Virginia. The news depressed Aughey more than his own plight. Two soldiers sat down near him and talked about the prison escape.

"I seed the cavalry start after 'em with ten all-fired packs of dogs. I'd give my wages for six months to ketch one of 'em. . . . Ole Bragg wouldn't stop at a thousand or two. Old Jordan he were bad flustered . . . cavortin' aroun' hollerin' out orders at the top of his voice, jest makin' the air blue with his cussin'. . . . I seed the officers put irons on 'em [the prison guards] an' they took 'em in ter that same jail the Tories had got out on."

The other said he bet that the escaped prisoners were plenty sharp and already with Tory friends not two miles from town. "Jack, you know the Clines and Kaverners—they'd die ter save a Union man."

"Them dogs 'll kum up with 'em. . . . They'll never make it to the Yankee lines." He came into the copse and broke a twig almost over Aughey's head, then jumped back. "Bill that was the biggest snake I've seen lately, a regular water-mocassin, but it got off inter the bushes. . . ." Aughey never moved.

That July 5 was the longest day in Aughey's life. When night

: *103* :

fell, he followed the North Star, friend of all Underground Railroad travelers, through dense woods that impeded his efforts. At Old Town Creek, he waded out on a fallen tree trunk, jumped off the end into water up to his armpits and clambered out on the far bank.

The water quenched his thirst, but he was hungry and tired and lay down at the foot of a large tree. The sun was rising when he woke. Badly upset at having lost so much time, famished and parched with thirst, he knocked at the door of a small cabin and a surly old man gave him a drink. He hastened away, but within a few feet was ordered to halt by two soldiers. One pointed a double-barreled gun at his belly.

"I know you, sir. I've heard you speak frequently. You are Parson Aughey, and I learned you had broken jail, and now you must return. My name is Don Burnham."

Burnham's father had been postmaster, and Don had been jailed twice for robbing the mails but had been freed when Mississippi seceded and had joined the Confederate army. "Parson . . . I was once in a tight place myself and would have been pleased to have found a friend to lend a helping hand." He said he would let Aughey go if he would pay him $250.

No sooner than had Aughey paid him than he jeered, "I was just playing off on you." He wished that every damned Tory was in hell. He led Aughey back through camp. Soldiers crowded about them, asking questions, so it took hours to get back to prison where he was questioned by General Jordan.

After saying that Malone would also be brought back soon by the dogs and cavalry, he took Aughey to a blacksmith to have fetters forged on. The blacksmith whispered to Aughey, "*Taisez-vous*," the Unionist password. "*Oui, oui*," replied Aughey. The blacksmith said he had never before manacled a man. Jordan drew his sword and told him to get on with it. "Iron him *securely*. . . . Make the bands and chain large and strong enough to prevent any chance of escape before he is hung." The bands, riveted on white hot, burned through Aughey's boots to the flesh, producing lifelong ulcers and scars.

"Iron, I understand," Aughey said to Jordan, "has become scarce in the South. You have given me an abundant supply."

Jordan told him he would be shot within the hour. Aughey wrote his wife, who was expecting another child, that he was dying because of his unswerving devotion to God and country. "I have no fear of death. I go trusting in Jesus. We will meet beyond the river."

Taken before General Braxton Bragg, Aughey asked to be shot instead of hanged. Bragg said he would be *hanged* in the presence of the army.

Back at Tupelo, the prisoners crowded around him. Malone had been captured but had escaped again through a backyard despite a hail of bullets. Two boys, having deserted after being held beyond their twelve-month enlistment period, were chained to the floor. Two officers came in, showed them their execution orders, big red letters reading CONDEMNED TO DEATH, undid their chains and marched them across the railroad tracks to the firing squad.

Aughey was informed that his execution would be as conspicuous as possible before two brigades, and his crimes would be commented upon by a full general. His trial would take place on Monday; he would be hanged on Tuesday. Aughey said that since he was to be hanged anyway, why not execute him on Monday and hold the trial on Tuesday. A Colonel Clive screamed at him, "Ingrate! Traitor! Wretch!" and threatened him with sword and pistol.

Two old men and four younger prisoners were taken out and shot for Union sympathies. They were forced to sit on the edge of a shallow hole and received three bullets each in the brain, three in the heart. Coffins were no longer used; executions were too numerous and too frequent.

These executions were going on all over the South, Aughey noted.

A reign of terror has been inaugurated. . . . Spies and informers in the pay of the rebel government prowl through the country using every artifice and stratagem to lead Unionists to incriminate themselves. . . . They are dragged to prison and to death. The cavalry dash through the country making daily raids, burning cotton, carrying off or wantonly destroying the property of loyal citizens. . . .

Aughey now considered his situation hopeless, but his fellow prisoners set to work to effect his escape again. With a long-handled spoon, filed sharp, his knife, and a file brought in by a Union soldier, they worked, two at a time, to cut the chain, while other prisoners crowded about to conceal what was being done. The chain was finally severed so it could be easily removed. General Jordan discovered that his irons had been tampered with and ordered that in the morning he be handcuffed and chained to the floor. "The gallows will not be cheated of their due."

His only chance was to escape that night. He paid eleven dollars for a shirt like the rebels wore and traded his light-colored trousers for dark ones. At ten o'clock that night, while the guards were being changed, he slipped through a hole in the porch and crawled to the north side. At the first aperture there were too many soldiers; at the second, a sleeping soldier suddenly sat up coughing and kept on for nearly an hour. At the third outlet, waiting for a good chance, he went to sleep and did not wake up until the cold and vermin made him uncomfortable. It was then three o'clock and soon would be daylight.

He crawled out, accidentally kicking a sleeping soldier in the head, and gradually made his way through clumps of soldiers, over sleeping bodies and past sentinels, and finally got into the woods. He knelt down and gave thanks to God.

After days more of frightful hunger and thirst, several more close brushes with bloodhounds and Confederate cavalry, a terrible storm struck, and Aughey staggered through the door of a roadside cabin two miles north of Albany in Tippah County. His face was bearded, his hair long and tangled, clothes tattered and muddy, and his leg bands clearly visible.

The woman inside threw up her hands in horror. "You are from Tupelo!" she gasped. She already knew of his escape. Their house had been searched several times, for they were only a few miles from a big army camp. She and her husband promised him every aid, and she hastened to set him down to cornbread and cold potatoes until she could prepare a meal. He wolfed down the food and became violently sick, but when the meal was served he ate everything. In the next room her little girl complained, "Ma, all I could get of that chicken was a tiny piece of wing. Wasn't that gentleman a hoss the way he et?"

His host, a blacksmith, was able to remove the iron bands, a painful business. They outfitted him in the husband's best suit and boots.

Several days later he reached the home of John Downing who agreed to guide him to the Federal lines. Scores of Unionist friends came to talk with him, though only a few days before the vigilantes had scalded a neighbor to death in front of his wife and children and had hung his body in a tree with a warning sign that anybody who took it down would receive the same treatment.

They passed on through several hamlets and had more narrow escapes. The last part of the way, Aughey went on foot to Rienzi. Federal sentinels took him to Colonel Z. Mizner, to whom he told his story and gave information as to the location and number of Confederate troops. For weeks he was a physical and mental wreck, and General Rosecrans sent two doctors to look after him. On his recovery Aughey enlisted as a chaplain. He often suffered painfully, especially from sores due to the leg irons, but he lived to a good age. His book *The Fighting Parson* was published in 1899.

Mississippi's Governor Pettus was a rough-hewn man, with an enormous head, a battleship nose and a mighty beard, from which he spat vaguely at a brass spittoon—a "tobacco ruminant," the London *Times* correspondent called him. His office was cluttered with papers and books, and he sat behind a plain table fronted by several old chairs and thundered out unalterable commands. He was an obstinate man, whose career had been made as a Secessionist firebrand, but his deep-grained states' rights ideas and his suspicions of Davis and the Confederacy, plus the serious problems confronting Mississippi and the uncertain temper of the people, caused him frequently to hinder rather than to promote the war effort.

He faced serious difficulties. Mississippi, though the tenth state in the Union in per capita wealth (most of it slaves, more numerous than whites) had no real money. The convention put a 50 per cent increase on all taxes to finance the war, but voted down a proposal to increase the tax on slaves from seventy-five cents to two dollars.

Nor did the state have any worth-while weapons. It had only squirrel guns collected from farmers, and no factories to produce war matériel. Besides the state prison shop, there were only four small textile mills in the whole state, not enough to provide for either the people or uniforms for recruits. The Military Board, instead of facing up to crucial war requirements, first decided on regulations for the color and cut, the braid and buttons of officers' uniforms. War was considered, in this twilight of chivalry, a grand parade rather than the grim business it soon became. In any event the powers-that-were thought it would all be over, and the North subdued, in a matter of months.

Mississippi, except for some meager subsistence farming, was a one-crop land, with little manufacturing, and in return for cotton sent to New Orleans (soon cut off by Federal troops), it brought in luxuries, necessities, and much of its food. Many people were hungry because of the 1860 crop failure, and their condition was to be worsened by an 1862 corn failure. Furthermore, King Cotton was dethroned almost at once, as banks failed and payments stopped in Louisiana. Louisiana and Tennessee bank notes at once became unredeemable. Even before the blockade, cotton piled up in warehouses and on the wharves. Mississippi produced a fourth of the entire cotton crop in the entire nation, and soon the 3,098 plantation owners were in dire straits, while smaller owners went bankrupt overnight.

Nor could the militia be clothed, fed, or paid wages. In spite of the widespread anti-secession feeling, the response was remarkable. The state had less than 100,000 white men between the ages of 16 and 60, and 78,000 of these enlisted or were drafted. Of these more than a third—27,500—died of disease or were killed, and at least 10,000 more were sent home maimed for life. A good portion of those were listed as "discharged, re-signed, or released," of whom, of course, perhaps 9,000 more were malingerers, soreheads, or deserters. The actual number of acknowledged desertions, one of the highest percentages of any state in the Confederacy, was 11,000. Only 18,750 men came straggling back to the state from Northern prisons, from Ap-pomattox, and elsewhere, at war's end, all through the long hot summer of 1865.

The governor soon had two hundred companies of troops, as the war began. Unable to feed, clothe, or pay them, he had to stop enlistments as early as May, for which he was promptly accused of throwing cold water on the war effort. In camp, hungry and hit by recurrent epidemics, the troops lay, without discipline, their morale declining, and grumbled for two long years. Had it not been for the herculean sacrifices of private citizens, who brought in food, clothing, and medicines, everywhere in scant supply, their condition would have been far worse.

Partly this long idleness was due to the governor's opposition to the Confederate authorities and partly his refusal to let the Confederate authorities take any arms out of the state. It was also due to the inability of the Confederacy to arm all the men.

A few companies were used to defend the Gulf counties, which the Confederacy had to protect, part were used to pro-tect Vicksburg before the Confederacy could fully garrison that crucial point on the river, and a good many, especially those having horses, were used to hunt down escaping slaves, to guard plantations against slave revolts, and later to hunt down deserters —these being the notorious "cavalry" which killed and looted the countryside.

The fear of slave uprisings kept much of Mississippi in a state of hysteria. Quite early in Adams County, where Natchez is lo-cated, forty Negroes were killed and many others maltreated and flung into jails. The Negro-hunting posses of Washington County and adjacent Pine Ridge Country, also along the river, were superactive throughout much of the war. Thousands of men who might otherwise have been at the front were kept busy nervously patrolling the countryside. Many plantations feared these armed patrols more than their own Negroes. To keep the Negroes from being wantonly killed, the owners confined them to the estate, though often under armed guard.

Pettus got pleas for arms for home guards from all over the state, which he was rarely able to meet and which he usually refused to heed. In this he was backed by Charles Clark, soon to replace him as war governor, who, in an exchange with the Natchez locals, called them "a band of old women with broom handles."

As plantation owners abandoned their plantations and left their slaves in the hands of private or state guards, fear mounted accordingly. While rumors spread, more Negroes were killed, often by the authorities or the troops, and the state records are cluttered with the petitions of plantation owners for remuneration. When the Federals occupied Vicksburg, Port Hudson, and Natchez, the Negroes became less docile. After the Emancipation Proclamation slaves began moving out en masse. In Lafayette County, they revolted and divided up mules and other property. Not all of them headed for Federal camps; many merely swarmed into cities and towns. John K. Butterworth, in his book *Confederate Mississippi*, describes how Jackson itself filled up with well-dressed, cigar-smoking, insolent Negroes lounging in all the streets.

From the start Pettus tried to keep military control in his hands and refused to permit the Confederacy to conscript or requisition any militia. He did nothing to back the suspension of *habeas corpus*. Granting such writs in behalf of deserters had become the chief activity of the judges, and Pettus insisted that all Mississippians had to be requisitioned for service through him. Furthermore the organization of the guard units reluctantly handed over to the Confederacy had to be kept intact, and indeed during the entire war only about 1,500 were ever transferred to other commands. Also, Mississippi officers had to remain in charge, a constant theme in all commands on both sides.

When anti-Secessionist James L. Alcorn became joint commander of the Mississippi militia, and headed the absorbed units that went to Kentucky, Jefferson Davis refused to recognize his commission. Alcorn returned to Mississippi breathing fire. He joined a mounting chorus of condemnation of Davis, calling him a "miserable, one-eyed, dyspeptic, arrogant tyrant . . ." drawing $25,000 a year in a cushioned seat, boasting of the future grandeur of a country he had ruined, its soil "wet with the tears of widows and orphans . . . bathed in the blood of a people once free but now enslaved. Oh, let me live to see him damned and sunk in the lowest hell."

Alcorn went back to Kentucky with independent units of sixty-day volunteers. They were scarcely armed, fed, or clothed, let alone trained, and the army called them the "bobtail sixty per cent militia." Conditions were so bad the men threatened to join other units or desert, and many did. They were particularly incensed over Alcorn's fellow commander, General George Reuben Davis, "a vain stuck-up illiterate ass . . . trying to play Henry of Navarre by wearing a feather in his hat." Nor were they appeased by his special Christmas ration of bad whiskey. Alcorn had returned to the front backed by a special legislative ruling that he had to be accorded the same rank as Confederate generals. He was soon outraged by orders from General Beauregard, which he considered an affront to himself and the militia, and he asked to resign, saying he would no longer be the tail of a kite dragging in the mud, "flopping and sloshing around —liable at any moment to have my brains knocked out."

This was a mere incident in the long controversy over the status of the militia carried on by Pettus and sometimes with even more acrimony by his successor, Charles Clark. The latter was an austere Delta planter and aristocrat. The South, said Clark, had nothing to fight with, except the finest boys in the world, not enough guns or ammunition to go around, and, he added in his inaugural address, "Let us, like the remnant of the heroic Pascagoulas, when their braves were slain, join hands together, march into the sea, and perish beneath the waters."

But it seemed more likely—this was early in 1863 before the fall of Vicksburg on July 4—that the ill-paid, ill-fed, idle militia would march to their homes to put in spring crops. Clark found himself hard-pressed to keep any sort of force mobilized, but because of the temper of the troops, their unwillingness to leave the state, and his own high-blown Mississippi dignity, he continued to fight all efforts of the Confederacy to get hold of them. Like Pettus, he insisted, but even more firmly, on separate commands and state control of all units. He did finally concede that militiamen, wanted by the Confederate draft, would be turned over to the army when their militia terms expired. This caused immediate wholesale desertions. He also conceded that the Confederate officers could command the militia for brief periods for definite objectives—but only within the state.

Bitter set-tos occurred and some almost led to armed struggle, as when Mississippi (militia) General Samuel J. Gholson resisted the orders of Confederate General G. R. Chalmers to state forces. One militia general was actually seized and incarcerated.

Governor Pettus finally agreed to let Gholson's forces be incorporated into the Confederate army, but as a unit. Neither officers nor men were to be shifted or changed. But Clark delayed in doing this, first withdrawing a thousand men to protect a session of the Legislature, then withdrawing six thousand cavalrymen to protect the state from deserters and possible Negro revolts. The Confederate Supreme Court decided in favor of the Confederacy on the transfer of the remainder—after Clark had threatened to use force to prevent their absorption. But he managed to hold up the transfer by insisting that the Confederacy first had to agree formally not to disturb the actual organization and also to pay all back pay. Until he took an appeal to the courts on the Supreme Court's decision, the forces, even if absorbed, could be used only to round up deserters and absentees within the state. He also proclaimed a blanket exemption from the draft for all elected officials and further protected them by having them join home guard units. Any arrested by the Confederate forces, he warned, would be given *habeas corpus*. He obstructed conscription efforts in every possible way.

The courts were already granting writs of *habeas corpus* at a wholesale rate. The army then began hustling conscripts out overnight, before they could reach a judge. This was particularly the case in northern counties, where civilian obstruction to the Confederacy was so strong that no conscription offices could even function. The state legislature passed a law that conscripts could be taken only after five days, and later lengthened this to ten.

Confederate impressment of goods and services caused increasing friction with both the people and the state authorities. Slaveowners protested loudly against the involuntary impressment of Negro workers, who were then not paid. Property seizures were widespread, without prompt payment and sometimes none at all. People were even ousted from their homes if the army wished to use them for offices or barracks—and sometimes to bring about shady transfers of title. The legislature promptly forbade house seizures. But officers, impressment agents, and many plain crooks posing as agents seized goods right and left. Anger grew so great and so vociferous that the Confederate War Department had to advise General Richard Taylor to put a stop to the scandalous outrages. At Canton, a captain was obliged to disgorge 600 pounds of stolen bacon.

There were loud and long disputes over trading with the enemy. The North was anxious for cotton and parts of Mississippi were almost starving. The trade was sanctioned and abetted by local, state, and even Confederate officials, though the graft and scandal were enormous. When the army began seizing men and wagons devoted to this almost open traffic, state officials—among them Judge Clayton—hotly demanded their release and an end to interference. The courts postponed cases or simply refused to sit to hear them or released prisoners. The provost marshals turned in many persons running the blockade, but apparently deliberately made it impossible to prosecute them by failing to make out a warrant for arrest, and providing no evidence or witnesses, so that any prisoners had to be released either by the commissioner or by the court. Rarely could a prosecutor be found who would press the cases. Practically the only ones punished were those arbitrarily subjected to martial law. Many women were engaged in contraband running. A few such were terrorized by vigilantes.

Actually the state government itself was actively engaged in dealing with the enemy. The first deal made was by Governor Pettus, who arranged to exchange cotton for salt with New Orleans. General John C. Pemberton, defender of Vicksburg, for a time also traded in cotton with Memphis and New Orleans. Likewise the Confederate Produce Loan Bureau itself bootlegged cotton to the enemy. Clark tried to get Confederate sanction for trade for essential supplies. This was not granted but he made a deal with the Commander of the Department and agents began openly bringing in supplies. The Confederate government finally recognized reality by putting the cotton trade in the hands of a single agent in Jackson. Though there was continual quarreling between him and his subordinates and the state government, some of the tension was eased. But this was late in 1864.

Both Pettus and Clark were strong Secessionists throughout, but equally strong states' rights men. They never became so openly involved in peace agitation as did Governor Brown of Georgia, but nevertheless they were obliged to oppose the Confederacy down the line on almost all crucial matters because of the increasingly rebellious attitude of the people and the peace groups, including stiff-necked, local patriots who put Mississippi's rights ahead of all else. The large pro-Union sentiment, and likewise the profiteering plantation owners, speculators, contrabandists, and food hoarders also made themselves heard. The 1862 elections had actually seen one out-and-out Unionist elected to the Confederate Congress. The swing was definitely toward the Whigs and ex-Whigs, mostly secret anti-Confederates, who throughout the struggle had stood staunchly for civil rights and openly condemned President Davis, General Pemberton, and other commanders. Many prominent Cooperationists were elected, and these and lesser peace elements infiltrated various government offices.

It became more and more difficult to administer the state as the Negroes became restive and fled in ever growing numbers toward the Federal lines or the cities. Ten thousand deserters roamed the swamps, the pine woods, and mountains, and came into towns to vote, gun in hand. They even "requisitioned" freight off the trains. The clamor for peace grew bolder, especially after the fall of Vicksburg.

Even before that, the Peace Society had become well organized throughout the state, indeed was rumored to have caused the surrender of that river city. Prominent men there promptly took the Union oath of allegiance. Many soldiers and most deserters became members, and when the Southern armies evacuated Corinth, by the time they reached Tupelo, nearly six thousand men were missing. After that, desertions mounted throughout the state. Everywhere, but especially in the northern and Gulf counties, people were openly or secretly taking the Union oath, many, of course, merely looking ahead to try to save their property or to trade more freely with the enemy.

In April, 1863, a Reverend James A. Lyon was saying there was no solution except for the people to rise in their majesty and arrange for an honorable and just reconstruction. In July in Jackson, Cooperationists such as J. O. Poindexter, William Yeger, and William Sharkey (later to become appointed Reconstruction governor) made plans for a new civil government, and a large meeting was held, with delegates from surrounding towns. Both Grant and Chalmers reported peace movements, and it was estimated that two-thirds of the northern county people had taken the Federal oath. The movement continued to grow. Lyon soon had hundreds of followers, and by 1864 a judge wrote President Davis that a large portion of the middle class, the more intelligent, and nearly the entire lower class were drifting to the Yankees. Observers in the southern counties reported strong peace sentiment, especially among the women, one saying that nine-tenths of the people were for peace and the Union. By this time the middle and lower counties were overrun with deserters and thieves, and local people lived under a virtual reign of terror. It was impossible to say who looted the state more, the deserters trying to survive—if not always to profit—or the vigilantes and "cavalrymen" who looted everything they could get their hands on. Just before the 1864 elections, even the official Jackson *Mississippian* came out for peace, and thereafter steps to organize a new government independent of the Confederacy and the existing state authorities were taken in numerous localities, quite openly.

The basic cause of desertions, peace sentiment, revived pro-Unionism, and the growing number of upper-class persons and politicians and leaders coming out for peace, was the growing realization, indicated in the last-ditch death drowning advocated by Governor Clark in his 1863 inaugural address, not merely that the war could never be won, but that things were so utterly rotten at home that they could not continue even if the Confederacy should be consolidated. Behind that basic realization, of course, was the general sad plight, restlessness, and despair of the common people. All during the war the gap between the rich and the poor had been widened, even though plenty of the more patriotic rich had also been ruined.

The state was being progressively looted on all levels, by speculating plantation owners, traders, food manipulators, army and militia officers, top politicians, on lower levels, by vigilantes, "cavalrymen," impressment agents, and deserters and draft dodgers. All this was on top of the heavy taxation and the terrible drain of the war effort, however fumblingly and incompetently it might be conducted. The state treasurer was charged with wholesale fraud and resigned. One commentator said that the politicians in the 1864 elections had become wolfish in their greed for office and jobs—the chance to amass goods illicitly.

The soldiers, too, clamored for peace, as they heard of the sufferings of their families. They were treated so poorly, that they could not be blamed, said one, for throwing down their guns. News from home came on top of little food, hardly any pay, ragged clothing, no shoes, no hospital or medical care, and the death toll from battle. Eleven entire Tishomingo County companies were wiped out at Forts Henry and Donelson. Soon thereafter Unionist bands roamed about at will, there as well as in neighboring Pontotoc and Itawaba counties. Confederate offices were closed down, conscription practically halted and taxes could not be collected.

Workers in Choctaw County, where there was considerable new Confederate industry, exchanged pledges with Northern workers not to fight each other, a disloyalty not discovered until 1864; but the flight of many workers to Yankeeland did not help the war effort either. In one of the Pearl River counties, one Joel Williams gave a dance for local deserters to celebrate the fall of Vicksburg.

Twenty-seven deserters came out of the woods in Leake County, armed with guns, pistols and Bowie knives to vote for Unionist candidates. The terror was working the other way now, for Confederates now feared retribution on *their* families and the pillaging of *their* properties. Even some staunch Confederates now began bellowing for peace. Everybody believed that life under the Union on any terms could not be worse than this. In Attala County, where the sheriff and prominent citizens had supported the Union from the very start of the war, at least one baby was named Abraham Lincoln, and a man rose in church, refusing to observe an official Davis fast day. Cavalrymen trying to round up deserters were often shot from ambush. Civil authorities made few or no arrests for disloyalty and refused to indict any indicated persons.

South of the open country, in the longleaf pine region, where the soil is so poor it will grow only a fourth of a bale of cotton per acre, where people had lived by floating an occasional log down the river or peddling peanuts in Mobile, where they went to church barefoot but were fiercely independent, Confederate authority crumbled. Whether there ever really was a

"Free State of Jonesia" is still a matter of hot dispute. If it existed, one witness said, it was set up "by eight men in a swamp." But there was enough authority apparently to issue paroles written on tree bark, and to raid Confederate supplies in Jason County and give them to poor families whose sons had refused to fight. They caused great terror among loyal Confederate farmers. It was said one band even raised the American flag over the Ellisville courthouse. Colonel Robert Lowrey, C.S.A., came in with bloodhounds and cavalry to hunt them down, but the local people fed the animals red pepper, destroying their powers of scent. Lowrey in desperation rounded up a few old men and boys and put them in jail, threatening to kill them. A man named Newton Knight had one of the most daring and best disciplined anti-Confederate bands in the state operating in this area.

But other counties were as overrun, perhaps more so. Jasper County was full of Irish Catholics who refused to fight. In Greene County the outlaw McLeod brothers cheered Abe Lincoln, strung up Negroes, and threatened to put strychnine into the local wells. Government depots were pillaged, and guardhouses, barns, and houses destroyed.

As in many counties, no taxes could be collected in Perry County, and the troops sent to put down marauders "frolicked and stole" too much, while the outlaw leaders led their men boldly into Augusta, the county seat, captured one Captain J. Bradford, gave him a "Federal parole" (which meant that if he continued in Confederate service he could be shot), then burned the jail, seized government supplies, and distributed them among the people. They told the townspeople they were going to have "peace or hell by August."

Copiah, Lawrence, Marion, and Pike counties were always full of disloyal elements, and matters steadily grew worse. Seditious handbills were frequently circulated, and it was boasted in Marion County that the people had long had their own anti-Confederate government.

The Gulf counties, the poorest in the state, were practically lost to the Confederacy at the outset, for people had to keep on trading with New Orleans or starve. Many people fled, and more prosperous folk and their goods were taken to New Orleans in Federal gunboats. So strong was Union sentiment that the Federals set up a regular recruiting office in Hancock County. These counties became a major center for deserters from all over the Confederacy, and any Confederate agent who was identified locally was likely never to live to talk about it.

In no other state or area, except possibly east Tennessee, was the war within a war more active, more virulent, more devastating, or more violent. From the beginning, Mississippi was a state ruled by terror and fear. Gradually the lawlessness on both sides was subdued by the pro-independent Unionist elements, and law was reestablished and shaped into new local self-rule, while the Confederate authority steadily crumbled. A new Mississippi was painfully being born. Unfortunately the Federal occupation and the imposed military government did not or was not able to make use of this popular upsurge. It did not take into account the fact that a reorganized society had to be the joint effort of both Negroes and whites. The basic issue and the consequences of emancipation were scarcely faced up to by anyone, either north or south.

7. Georgia and Brown

The Know-Nothing movement, backed by the influential Augusta *Chronicler and Sentinel,* had lifted its greasy locks in Georgia in mid-1854, with an attack on the 2,200 "foreign-owned" grog shops, and had won political control of a number of large cities. The Know-Nothings came, Alex Stephens said, "toting their own skillets," joining no party. They also came at a time when the Whig Party was going to pieces. The Whigs rallied with the Union Democrats, another splinter group, into the short-lived Consolidated Union Party. Secessionism versus unionism was already a nose-pummeling issue, but the Know-Nothings, though Federalists of a sort, brought in a new element of confusion by their conspiratorial strong-arm methods. But Herschel V. Johnson, an anti-Secessionist and a pre-Civil War Democratic boss in the state, ran for reelection as governor in 1855 and literally whipped the Know-Nothings off the hustings.

In 1857 Joseph E. Brown, a dark-horse candidate from northern Georgia, a Southern Rights Democrat, was jockeyed into the candidacy for governor in a deadlocked Democratic convention by the backstage politicians. "Who the devil is Joe Brown?" Senator Robert Toombs wanted to know.

The leading papers blossomed out with laudatory biographies. Brown, it seemed, was a man of severe, continued, untiring personal application and laborious research, a most profound and able man—novel and unlikely qualities in any politician. He loved the Union for the sake of the states, not the states for the sake of the Union, double-talk with which politicians fertilize votes. Pollard of Virginia, denouncing Brown, was to say sourly, a bit later: "Union! That motto of ambitious politicians and the favorite theme of demagogues." The paraphrase "the glorious Union" was an unnatural tumor. But the more conservative Southerners, such as Pollard, and those not so conservative, had far sillier catch-words.

Brown, a former plowboy, a strong Baptist, was married to the daughter of a Baptist preacher, a sect that in the South had long since lost the noble tolerance which had impelled its American founding by the notable Roger Williams of Rhode Island. However, Brown straddled the important temperance issue, for which he was an intemperate advocate, by declaring that what was needed was not legislation but moral suasion—an issue-dodging phrase even in those days. Later, during the war, he shut down all distilleries, including those owned and operated by the Confederate government, saying the grain was needed for food, and he made it a crime to sell or give whiskey to either state or Confederate regular troops.

His most pronounced characteristics, according to Louise Bates Hill's biography, were the following: he was a vote-getter, an able executive, and a money-maker. He had to sell a pair of oxen in order to attend Calhoun Academy, but later, serving an unprecedented four terms as governor and by means of his postwar alignment with the Reconstruction forces, he used his political assets, apparently without directly pilfering the treasury, to make millions of dollars.

Tall, thin, awkward, he had a large head and a big determined mouth that uttered plain homespun truths with little elegance or tact, though with great sophistry. He was never appalled by his own twisting of the facts—a good requirement for a politician. Combative by nature, incredibly obstinate, he never backed down in the face of legislative defeats, the antagonism of the press, or general public abuse—and the votes rolled in with ever bigger majorities.

In that 1857 election his chief opponent was the Know-Nothing candidate, Benjamin H. Hill, a brilliant speaker, whose sharp-edged mind deserved a better platform and cause. Hill easily mastered Brown in joint debates, which the Democrats promptly terminated, and Toombs, with his great mane of dark hair, a greater orator than Hill, took Brown under his wing on a tour of the pine-torch circuit, until the latter could make a more creditable showing. He was elected by a modest majority.

The shocked plantation elite looked down their noses at him from inherited legislative seats, and he soon had to knock some heads together. The 1857 depression was bearing down, and he refused to dance to the tune of the banks then tottering on the brink. They were guilty, he said, of a triple commercial, moral, and legal crime, and he did not intend to let them dictate the terms of their own pardon. He vetoed their proposed bill, took away the charters of offenders and forced payment to creditors. Screams of anguish rose from the press. A Savannah paper accused him of poisoning the minds of the laboring class. "We have been trying to find out who Brown is, now we know, he's a d—— fool!"

The legislature overrode his veto of the bankers' bill by 4 to 1, but great mass meetings shouted support for him, so he began rigorously and boastfully enforcing the existing banking code. He refused to accept bank bills for money owed the state. He drew blood.

He next cleaned up the scandalous graft in the state-owned railroad, firing personnel widely and appointing Baptists, and turned it into a big profit-making enterprise that provided a large share of state revenues. He pushed education on every level.

As secession roared closer, he rehabilitated and expanded the militia. He built up the state shipping fleet, bought arms from Europe, and started factories to manufacture military equipment. He purchased nearly every privately owned gun in the state and, when war came, Toombs noted, he had more guns than the whole Confederacy, which, according to Davis, then had only 15,000 new rifles and 120,000 old model rifles in bad repair, mostly seized from Federal arsenals. By May 4, 1861, Brown had organized, armed, and drilled six regiments and two battalions and by the end of the year had fifty regiments. By tact and restraint he pulled most pro-Union mountain folk, at least temporarily, into supporting the Confederacy.

As early as November 7, 1860, he called for a secession convention and informed the world that King Cotton made the South invincible. He asked for the immediate seizure of the local property of any Northern states that had violated the Fugitive Slave Law or that had freed the slaves of Southerners passing through their territories, and confiscated and ordered sold all New York State vessels in Georgia waters when that Northern state arrogantly confiscated a Georgia arms shipment in transit. New York backed down at once.

On January 2, 1861, his militia took over Fort Pulaski at Savannah, and he was given a big torchlight parade. He then telegraphed the governors of Mississippi, Alabama, and Florida to seize all Federal forts at once. Florida did not feel its forces were sufficient to take over Pensacola and asked Alabama to do it. At once Brown wired Alabama's governor asking if he had done so.

But not until January 19 was the convention able to override the bitter Johnson-Stephens opposition to secession and enable Georgia to leave the Union.

After the Confederacy was set up in Montgomery, Brown did not hasten to send Georgia troops in answer to the Secretary of War's call, but negotiated as to their status. He would send only full regiments, in which all senior officers would be named by himself, and junior officers would be elected by the troops. Enlistment had to be for only twelve months, not the duration. Other Southern states took similar positions. Most of the governors finally gave in to Richmond's orders, but not Brown. Davis later called him a foe of the South.

His conditions made it impossible for Davis to organize an effective army. But only after Secretary Randolph capitulated did Brown send a thousand men to garrison Fort Pulaski and two well-trained regiments to Richmond. The next contingents, he said, would be of brigade strength under the same conditions. This would further limit Confederate control and mobility, and the Secretary said that no units larger than regiments would be accepted. The interchange became acrimonious. Losing his temper, the Secretary warned Brown that if he refused he would regret it. Davis, who could not afford to lose the richest, most powerful state in the Confederacy, smoothed down Brown's ruffled feathers and accepted his terms, then and later, except in shipping matters.

Brown further ruled that all direct volunteers to the Confederate army were part of the militia. No Georgia men, he insisted, were going to be commanded by non-Georgia officers. He warned the legislature that Davis was dying to get full control of the military forces of the Confederacy, both the sword and the purse, to set up a military dictatorship under which the people and the states would be helpless.

He flatly refused to permit his militia units sent north to take any arms or ammunition out of the state. When his own Floyd Sharpshooters evaded the order by secretly expressing their arms north ahead of them, he angrily demanded that the Confederacy ship them back. Unable to arm the Georgia recruits sent him, General Albert Sydney Johnston had to retreat ignominiously from Bowling Green. Later there was an ugly hassle over powder at the Augusta Confederate arsenal, which the commanding officer refused to turn over to the militia. Brown then refused to issue any supplies to Confederate officers and shut down the state munition plants. After another hot interchange, most of the powder was handed over to Brown.

As Brown became more and more obstreperous, other states began imitating him, especially North Carolina, Mississippi, Alabama, and Florida.

Nor was Brown's obstruction limited to military matters. Jealous of the state railroad (now providing a large share of Georgia's revenues), when the generals tried to take equipment and rolling stock for the Tennessee front, Brown said if necessary he would use his own military force to prevent it. Again the Richmond authorities had to back down. During the entire war he would not allow the Confederate government to touch anything belonging to the road or utilize rolling stock outside the state. He refused to let it be absorbed when Davis made a desperate effort to unify the Southern transportation system, which had progressively broken down. Time and again, under Brown's orders, the line gave priority over military supplies to goods for Georgia's own use. In 1863 when General Braxton Bragg, holding Atlanta, said he would use force to get his supplies over it, Brown threatened to shut down operations entirely. Again Davis hastened to back down. The same crisis arose with General Johnston after the fall of Chattanooga.

In spite of the constant quarrels, Georgia—on its own terms—supplied forty regiments and three battalions to the Confederacy, a notable record. But Brown was always demanding troops sent back to protect the Georgia coast or for other emergencies, real or imagined, and the Georgia desertion rate was high, though others were higher.

If he begrudged everything shipped out of Georgia, nevertheless Brown promoted more wartime production and started more factories than did any other state governor, which was made possible because Georgia was the most developed of the Southern states. She had more miles of railroad than almost any state in the North. Brown was able to produce enough shoes and blankets, even a surplus, and he kept consumer prices down.

To this end he seized all tin and salt to maintain low prices and equitable distribution. Georgia had no salt production and he spent great sums to get that precious commodity from Europe or from Virginia, the only important source in the Confederacy, until new rich deposits were found in Louisiana (which soon passed into Federal hands). He even sent a state railroad engine to get salt from the big Virginia mine, whereas North Carolina and other states were cut off. Every Georgia family was guaranteed a supply at low, nearly prewar prices, and could buy more at higher prices, but well under the fantastic open market price. Unlike much Southern meat, Georgia's products were not lost for lack of salt to preserve them.

Brown's obstructions favored Georgia at all times, without regard for the war effort. They were motivated in part by his personal detestation of Davis, his fear of centralized dictatorship, and his fierce loyalty to traditional civil and states' rights. His loud, outspoken criticisms and his reiterated charges of dictatorship, made most Richmond officials feel that he was jeopardizing the war effort, and that his actions at all times were close to treason. They constituted, whether consciously or not, part of the war within a war, and they integrated all sorts of individual and group resistance to both Davis and the Confederate war effort.

As already noted, he shouted to the whole world that conscription was a betrayal of the secession movement intended to destroy the rights of man and the sovereignty of the states, a dastardly scheme by Davis to get control of local troops and appoint all officers in his over-all effort to establish a military dictatorship. At one fell swoop, Brown said, conscription struck down the sovereignty of the states, trampled upon the constitutional rights and personal liberty of the citizens, and armed the President with imperial power. He was not going to allow Georgia's troops to be disorganized or her state government to be destroyed.

He told Davis pointblank that he would not allow state employees or officials to be conscripted and called out the militia to resist. The Secretary of War was then obliged to make similar exemptions in all the states, though no other governor exempted such a large percentage of the population. The Secretary of War told the press ruefully he had yielded, "just as you or I would have yielded to a madman who stood over a barrel of powder with a lighted match."

Brown's anger was uncontrollable when, on September 27, 1862, the draft age was raised to 45. It would drag away men needed in field and factory. No act of the President of the United States had struck such a blow at constitutional liberty, he said. The issue was the preservation of the states or else a consolidated military despotism. He refused to permit further conscription until the matter had been passed on by the legislature, not then in session, especially as the Confederacy had broken faith in its pledges to Georgia's twelve-month enlistment men. He demanded they be released at once. His defiance coincided with major defeats of Lee, Bragg, and Van Dorn.

The state Supreme Court ruled the Conscription Act legal. Brown said angrily that its decision was due to heavy pressure. He widened still further the categories of persons not subject to the draft. In this measure he was backed up by the legislature. With some slyness, a newspaper noted that, in his effort to get everybody exempted, he had somehow neglected to include the Attorney General, the Solicitor General, and the Masters of Chancery—not that they ran much risk of being called.

At every turn Brown protested to Richmond concerning its efforts to enforce the draft, denounced the arrogance of the non-Georgia officers sent in—"thousands of young officers in gold lace and brass buttons." His feelings were exacerbated still more when in February, 1864, the draft age was extended from 17 to 50 years. At all times his ill feelings about the draft were accentuated by the favoritism displayed in behalf of the wealthy and the slaveowners.

The officer in charge of Georgia conscription wrote to General Cobb, according to Louise Bates Hill:

> The Executive . . . and his officials and partisans, aided by a few prominent and influential public men in the State, have persistently labored to oppose the execution of these laws and to create public opposition not only to their then execution, but commendatory of their evasion.

Compliance became dishonorable.

Davis was bitter when Hood was beleaguered at Atlanta, because of the many Georgia exemptions. Fifteen thousand men could have been raised, he claimed, but considering the heavy backlash of desertions at that time, it probably could have been accomplished, if at all, only by the use of ferocious military coercion, and it is also doubtful whether they could have been armed.

Pollard, the Richmond editor, who also hated Davis, charged

that Brown had raised a false clamor by appealing to political prejudices against a centralization of power in order to marshal old-time anti-secession elements in Georgia, Tennessee, and North Carolina. The net result, he stated, was to weaken and betray the Confederacy.

At one time it was thought Brown had personal military ambitions and that he could be pried loose from Georgia by commissioning him as a Confederate general with a large force. Though many a blundering politician—provided he was a member of Davis' wing of the Democratic Party—had been elevated to high rank with no experience whatever, General Lee put a crimp in this proposal with the curt sentence that he had no knowledge of Brown's military abilities.

Many Georgians were appalled by Brown's opposition to Davis. In general the newspapers and the legislators lambasted him, but he generally got the laws he wanted and in the 1863 election rolled up a bigger majority than ever. He had looked after the poor Georgians, reduced their taxes, lowered prices on necessities, and in many ways had lightened war hardships in a manner done in no other state.

His opposition to Confederate financial legislation and restrictions on state shipping was quite as ferocious and determined as his opposition to conscription. The Confederacy had stumbled along for the first two years in bankruptcy, depending chiefly on exportation of cotton, which brought in less and less because of the blockade and piled-up surpluses. There had been only $27,000,000 to begin with in the Confederate treasury, and credit in Europe was soon wiped out, making it difficult to buy arms or supplies. But no other tax was levied until 1863, when the Impressment Law of March 26 permitted the army to seize needed supplies. It was arrogantly imposed, and the prices paid were far below the market level. Both farmers and speculators, holding commodities on an ever soaring market, were furious. Davis said, six months later, that the fear of impressment had brought about lower prices because of quick sales. Since prices kept soaring, this was not, somehow, convincing.

Brown's hostility to the Impressment Law made enforcement difficult. He took measures to prevent supplies from being delivered outside the state, and the central government found it almost impossible to feed Bragg's army in his siege of Chattanooga. Secretary of War Seddon's pleas to Brown were disregarded. If the government would pay market prices, retorted Brown, it would not have to seize produce.

In his November, 1863, message, he was savage about the illegalities of Confederate agents engaged in "moral robbery" and "plundering." He suggested ten-year imprisonment and thirty-nine lashes on the bare back when authority was exceeded. He secured a state Supreme Court decision that the government had to pay the market price. Just before its final downfall, the Confederacy gave in and ordered payment everywhere at the current (grossly inflated) prices.

Brown demanded heavy direct taxation, but when such a law was passed on April 24, 1863, it did not tax land or slaves, the chief wealth of the South, but rather farm products by a tax-in-kind, a tithe. This unfair burden on the farmers would be the winding sheet of the government, declared Toombs. There was no census to make the law equitably operative, declared Brown.

By early 1863 the Richmond government was sinking under the flood of its own treasury notes. The states had also issued their own notes. Finally the Confederacy asked the states to guarantee a bond issue—$200,000,000 of 30-year bonds at 6 per cent. Vice-President Stephens, who by that time had retired from Richmond and had said himself that the Confederacy was bankrupt, initiated a vigorous campaign to prevent state endorsement. Governor Brown took the same position in his message to the legislature. It would injure the credit of those states that had managed their financial affairs better than others. Georgia was entitled to the benefits of her wise management and far-reaching statesmanship. Furthermore it was unconstitutional and would strengthen the central government. Power once usurped, he told the people, is never relaxed but at the point of the bayonet. The legislature voted to refer the matter to the people. This was never done.

By December, Confederate currency amounted to $600,000,000 and was worth scarcely ten cents on the dollar. Prices skyrocketed and speculation thrived. In his 1864 message, Brown was still damning the Confederacy for its unsound fiscal policy and bad faith.

He clashed head-on with the Confederacy with respect to Georgia shipping. Cotton was selling in the South for about 6 cents a pound; in London at 60 cents a pound, a big bonanza for blockade runners who often made $100,000 or more each trip. They brought back compact luxuries instead of bulky arms.

The Richmond government had only four small vessels of its own, but the states had gone into the traffic in a big way, and British companies were operating a large fleet of swift vessels, often former Hong Kong–China opium runners. Thus the South was getting little for its cotton, was being drained of gold, and deprived of new weapons; ostentatious luxury in society passed beyond all decent bounds, demoralizing for the ill-fed and ill-clothed soldiers and civilians. In the fall of 1863, by Richmond's decree, ships were required to set aside one-third to one-half their cargo space for government goods. Even so, the government still had to pay the exorbitant freight rates, from $500 to $1,000 a ton, and, until it organized sales and purchasing offices abroad, continued to get only 6 cents to 10 cents a pound for cotton. During the first nine months of 1863, 100,000 bales reached England and sold there for $20,000,000, but it is doubtful if the Confederacy netted a million dollars. Even so, the Confederacy was able to buy a few ships and get torpedo boats to fight the blockade, as well as more munitions, arms, and some medicine.

For several weeks, precisely when Grant's and Sherman's campaigns were beginning, all vessels went on strike. Thereafter the regulations were evaded. Since vessels owned or leased by the states or railroads were exempted from Davis' regulations, blockade-runners sold shares to Confederate railroads and the states.

Not until February, 1864, did the government attempt to remedy this by prohibiting the importation of luxuries, and said that all exports had to be licensed. Also, lower shipping rates were arbitrarily set.

On March 1, the very day these more drastic regulations went into effect, Brown purchased shares in shipping companies and chartered four vessels directly. He also pushed a test case. He loaded the *Little Ada*, a privately owned vessel, with state cotton. The Confederate government refused clearance. At once Brown telegraphed other governors, stating that the Confederate government had refused to permit the states to export their own products and asked them to protest. In the end, the Confederate Congress lifted all regulations on shipping. The speculators and Governor Brown had won. The end of the Confederacy was close at hand.

Next to conscription, Governor Brown's most concentrated attack on the Confederate Government—and this at a time when its cause was clearly lost—was against the first and second suspension of the writ of *habeas corpus*. The ramrod of this resistance in Georgia was Vice-President Stephens, but Toombs joined in also, saying that Davis and his "Janissaries" were using the pretext of public danger to further their selfish and infamous schemes. Certainly there was strong popular and official opposition to the measure in every Confederate state, but nowhere more than in North Carolina and Georgia. Similar opposition to Lincoln's earlier suspension of this right occurred in the North, but the issue was more serious in the South, for it was fast losing the war. The agitation against it was linked with an ever growing peace movement and wholesale desertion.

Though the first suspension in 1862 was not applied to groups, General Bragg, on his own initiative, declared martial law in Atlanta, something Stephens declared he had no more authority to impose than did a street-walker. Before the legislature Brown branded Bragg's high-handed usurpation as subversion of the government and sovereignty of the state. The War Department promptly repudiated Bragg's order and forbade military officers to proclaim martial law or to suspend the writ without authority from the President.

The first suspension of the writ expired February 15, 1863, but in the dark hours of 1864, it was again imposed. Promptly, Brown convened a special session of the legislature to consider, among other things, the new Conscription Act, the suspension of the writ, and peace. He informed that body he intended to keep on repelling every encroachment by the central government. The suspension law was an act to authorize the President to make "illegal and unconstitutional arrests," to drag people from their homes at midnight with armed force to be examined in the "Confederate Star Chambers," a bold stride toward military despotism. The state legislatures should stop this. Confederate independence would mean little if constitutional liberty were lost. As for peace, the war could not be terminated by force of arms but only through negotiations and a plebiscite North and South. He sent copies of his message and the resolutions to every county clerk and sheriff in the Confederacy.

Opposition newspapers in Georgia, South Carolina, and elsewhere labeled him a demagogue, madman, marplot, firebrand, as wrong-headed, contentious, and troublesome, Brown gave no ground. Though opposed also by a group of Confederate wheelhorses such as Howell Cobb and Bergman H. Hill, he had the legislature invite Vice-President Stephens to speak. Stephens argued that the best way to repel the enemy was to make people's rights and liberties secure. He attacked conscription: brains, he said, must do something as well as muskets. The law meant that no one between the ages of 17 and 50 could tan leather, make shoes, grind grain, shoe horses, or repair harness without the President's permission. He recited the history of *habeas corpus* in England, and referred to the pernicious French royal *lettres de cachet*. The suspension denied any person conscripted improperly, as well as any others arrested, the chance to get their cases adjudicated by the courts, and he cited numerous examples of underage or overage men improperly drafted who had suffered harrowing experiences. He warned of the dictator's siren song, of independence first and liberty afterwards. Let both be cherished as co-ordinate, co-existent, co-equal, and forever inseparable, he closed.

Brown's enemies charged that he had sold to legislators imported cotton-textile cards, worth sixty dollars, for ten dollars; that he had exchanged their Confederate money dollar for dollar with state money, worth twice as much and that thirty-six votes were venally bought in this manner.

Even so the legislature tried to sidestep the issue by calling for quick adjournment on a Saturday. The governor said that if the anticonscription, antisuspension, and peace resolutions were not passed by then he would call them back on Monday. And so the resolutions in favor of *habeas corpus*, slightly amended, squeaked through before Saturday midnight, and, somewhat watered down, the conscription and peace resolutions also.

Extension of the law suspending *habeas corpus* then died in the Confederate Congress, but Brown was still complaining on February 15, 1865, that citizens were being arbitrarily arrested by the military and held without trial. Loyal citizens without passes were arrested, while Federal spies could travel over the thoroughfares at their leisure, he wrote.

Brown was a vociferous advocate for peace. The Southern peace movement, he alleged, was paralleled in the North, where "Butcher" Grant was being cursed by 100,000 grieving families. By 1864, Greeley of the *Tribune* actually feared armed insurrection and that Lincoln would be defeated in the November elections. But Sherman's seizure of Atlanta put victory in sight, and the Northern peace movement collapsed. Lincoln's reelection was assured.

But well before this, Brown had believed that peace was possible and that a battlefield solution was unlikely. To head off Stephens, Brown, and other leading peace advocates, Davis initiated two peace negotiations, which he knew beforehand would fail, for he insisted that the Confederacy had to be recognized as independent—Lincoln could not and would not accept this—and insisted that the South could be readmitted to the Union only state by state. The negotiations, Brown claimed, had never been put before the Southern people; people in the North had never even been told there had *been* any negotiations. It was the duty of the Confederate government to keep the peace efforts alive.

He claimed the South should make peace as soon as the enemy would recognize the great fundamental principles of the Declaration of Independence. After every victory, the Confederacy should renew its offers. If the offers were declined by Lincoln, the Northern people would hurl from power those who deny the fundamental principles upon which their own liberties rest. Make the proposition again and again, he urged. He called for a peace plebiscite in the Confederacy and the Union border slave states.

"Let both governments adopt this mode of settlement . . . and the ballot box will soon achieve what the sword cannot accomplish." But to his chagrin, his own militia passed resolutions against his peace stand. The George T. Anderson brigade accused him of being ready to sacrifice everything to his own self-aggrandizement and personal ambition, and said he had prostituted the dignity of his high office to unholy ambition. This was early in 1864.

Benjamin Hill called his peace efforts and his opposition to Confederate measures twin falsehoods and treachery to promote division and the belief that surrender was inevitable. It was clear that Brown had never wanted war, was soon out of step with it, that he wanted peace without victory, and that he was willing to forego Confederate recognition or independence. All he wanted was to obtain as much recognition of state sovereignty and state control over local institutions as possible—in other words, the prewar status.

Boldly he called for a plebiscite in each Confederate state to amend the constitution so as to permit a convention of all states *North and South*. President Davis, he implied, was the one obstacle to a negotiated peace, and he told the legislature that Confederate independence with centralized power, without state sovereignty and constitutional liberty would be very little better than subjugation. The longer the war lasted, the less chance there would be to prevent such evils. Brown persisted, and went even farther.

The war could not be terminated by the sword, he contended once more, but was likely to continue until both sides were exhausted with no rewards for anybody. Both governments, North and South, would have usurped the powers of absolute despots. Posterity could never pay the mountains of debt. Hundreds of thousands more men would be slain and millions of women and children widowed, orphaned, and poverty-stricken. Civil laws would give way to robbery and murder.

Only the people in their aggregate capacity as sovereign states could force the two governments to stop fighting and negotiate a settlement on the principles of 1776—as already put forth by the resolutions passed in the Georgia legislature. The Southern states had seceded from the Union; they had the same right to secede from the Confederacy, and he proposed immediate peace conventions of all Southern states to abolish the Confederate States of America. All of them, North and South, should secede and, as sovereign, equal and independent states, call a convention.

But on November 12, the legislature voted down the Brown-Stephens resolutions and reaffirmed allegiance to Davis. Alexander Stephens then rushed to Richmond to try to get Davis impeached for incompetence, bad judgment, and despotism. He rushed a Senate resolution calling for a peace convention of all the states, details to be arranged jointly by peace commissions from both sides. It seemed possible the resolutions might pass.

But a supposedly authorized Northern peace envoy, Francis P. Blair, arrived in Richmond to discuss terms. Stephens claimed that his visit was deliberately arranged by Davis to head off peace. Certainly Davis outsmarted Stephens by appointing the Vice-President as a member of a three-man commission at a joint North-South peace conference at Hampton Roads. Others claimed, probably falsely, that Davis was dazzled by a Blair proposal that if he would make peace, he would be put in charge of a great combined army for the conquest of Mexico.

But on February 15, 1865, Brown convened a special legislative session to call for a convention, depose Davis, or else secede from the Confederacy. Governor Vance of North Carolina feared such a convention would result in counterrevolution and bloodshed and asked Brown to call it off, since North Carolina would certainly follow Georgia's lead. Let Davis go ahead with his peace parley, argued Vance, before we take matters into our own hands or inaugurate revolutionary measures.

However, Brown told the legislature that the whole body politic was diseased and called for a commander-in-chief of the armies who would depose Davis. He asked that Georgia commissioners be sent to all Confederate states to get them to call special conventions for this purpose. He declared that Davis' suspension of *habeas corpus* and his establishment of a one-man authority to decide who could publish a newspaper, preach a sermon, doctor the sick or teach the young, constituted complete usurpation and the end of all liberty. He harangued the militia in similar vein.

A few days later Lee surrendered and the end was at hand. For nearly three weeks more, Brown helped hurry the struggle to its inevitable end. Even with the obvious before their eyes, the patent evidence that the war was really over, the legislature listened to a ferocious denunciation of Brown ("treason most foul and damning . . . little better than Catiline or Benedict Arnold") and voted overwhelmingly—with only two members opposing—in favor of Davis and for a vigorous prosecution of the war.

It was too late, and they were talking to a void.

8. The Negroes

The Negroes were growing disaffected, reported General J. W. Phelps from Louisiana in mid-1862. Unless a proper policy was adopted soon, there was likelihood of a violent revolution that would engulf a million Negroes and could not be controlled. It was becoming more imminent every day. Four million whites, he estimated, would be impelled, because of their growing miseries, to join with the blacks. Already they had desperate leaders, and he cited the "traitor" Mumford who had "swung the other day for trampling on the Confederate flag."

Nearly a year later, the Union General Weitzel, on an up-river campaign, refused to command any Negro troops and informed his superior, General Benjamin F. Butler, that a "heart-rending" black insurrection was brewing, that (white) women and children were panic-stricken. He proposed to halt his advance to prevent this.

"Absurd!" stormed Butler. Weitzel himself had just reported the brutal murder by the local Southern militia of seven Vermont prisoners forced to dig their own graves. Was that not as heart-rending as prospective insurrection? According to Weitzel, Mrs. Bragg, wife of the Confederate general, was one of the terrified women, and Butler reminded him that if General Braxton Bragg were at home protecting her, he would not at that moment be ravaging the homes "of our brothers in Kentucky." He ordered Weitzel to demand the surrender of all Confederate forces in return for a guarantee that law and order would be maintained.

In spite of widespread fear by Southern whites of Negro revolt, there were no mass uprisings, perhaps because so many troops were always present, and in many states armed militia guards were detailed to protect plantations. Negro work gangs were locked up at night under guard, both in and out of the army. Even so, Negro plots, real or imaginary, were discovered in nearly every state. Slaves were executed and mass arrests made. Such a plot was reported in Monroe County, Arkansas, between Little Rock and Memphis, where it was alleged slaves intended to murder white men and, if resisted, women and children also. Many were hung; many arrested. Similar episodes occurred in Washington and Adams counties in Mississippi and through much of the Black Belt. Negroes who wandered off the plantation to see friends or their families on other plantations, to make purchases or go fishing, were apt to be wantonly killed by Confederate cavalry units, by Negro-hunting militiamen or by vigilantes, particularly in Mississippi and Alabama. Many slaveowners ordered their Negroes not to leave the plantation. But as food grew scarce and the plantation was not able to provide for the slaves, as the spirit of independence and new freedom began to spread, particularly after the Emancipation Proclamation, and as Federal armies drew nearer, the exodus began. In some cases, especially where no more cotton could be grown and not enough food could be provided, the plantation owners themselves threw the Negroes out. The great dislocation due to the cotton crisis and the war set hundreds of thousands of Negroes adrift to roam the highways and flood the towns, often suffering great miseries.

There was a hierarchy among the Negroes. On top were the favored house servants, nursemaids, coachmen, gardeners. In some instances they were the offspring of the masters. Some came to enjoy positions of confidence, buying and selling, and handling large sums of money. Many were literate and enjoyed most of the amenities of the Big House. They cared for the children and, as they grew up, instructed them in upper-class etiquette and good manners.

This group was, with exceptions, loyal to the end. Some body servants accompanied their masters to the front lines and risked their lives to aid and protect them. One servitor was killed taking his master's sword through the fire of battle. Others rounded up new horses to replace those shot, or they bound up their master's wounds.

Another group also had some superior privileges: the skilled artisans, repairmen, caretakers of barnyard animals, straw bosses and muleteers. A few of these were also literate. Many were hired out in towns and elsewhere with considerable profit to their owners.

The largest number of slaves, of course, were ignorant field hands, who toiled from dawn to dark, though often they had leisure time. Most were dressed in rags, often barefoot, ate poorly and lived in the filthiest hovels. They did enjoy some medical care. Plantations frequently hired doctors by the year to look after slaves.

Free Negroes, of whom there was an ever increasing number, if they did not drift North, remained largely in cities and towns, doing odd jobs but rarely living well and always apprehensive lest they be re-enslaved or suffer physical violence. They had little legal protection in case of difficulties. Usually they were not allowed to testify in court.

For most Negroes the idea of freedom, however they might crave it, was a fearful prospect. Their roots were in the soil; their world was the plantation, where they could at least survive. The free wage system existed only to a limited degree in the towns; there were few factories, and Negroes were allowed only the most menial jobs. Unless they could seize the land as their own, a possibility that scarcely occurred to them, they could find no economic security. To revolt as individuals or even en masse appeared to bring no opportunities, merely frightful reprisals. Yet little by little, as the conflict went on, the Negroes, who were the basic cause of the war, did more and more in behalf of emancipation. They helped Unionist refugees, they guided armed outlaw bands, they served as spies, messengers, and informants and helped escaping deserters. Those dislocated even before the war ended hunted for niches of safety and many became accustomed to self-reliance. In the Memphis, Vicksburg, Natchez, and Little Rock areas a large share of the 700,000 blacks were tossed like autumn leaves to rustle up and down the fields and highways or to take refuge in United States army camps. Even before the Emancipation Proclamation, tens of thousands were able to enlist in the Northern army, where they fought valiantly for what they believed spelled freedom and the new order.

Much of the fear of slaveowners arose from the fact that they had to leave their womenfolk behind, inadequately protected. It turned out that many of these long-sheltered souls were able to run the plantations better, get more work done, and enjoy more respect than had their absent mates. But the gnawing fear of Negro violence was there from the start and never abated. The owners knew the stories of earlier revolts: the terrible 1812 Denmark Vesey conspiracy in Charleston; the 1831 Nat Turner uprising on Southampton, Virginia, plantations—led by a man with coals on his lips and glory in his face, whose prophecies frightened even the whites. The long chronicle of such revolts has scarcely been narrated. Then, near-panic shook slaveowners over Osawatomie John Brown's October 16–18, 1859, raid at Harpers Ferry, culminating in his call to all Negroes to strike off their chains. The slaveowners held their collective breath until he walked out of jail to the gallows on December 2, with a radiant face and the step of a conqueror.

If slaveholders' fears—and others shared those fears—were never actually realized, they were powerful enough seriously to undermine the war effort. Large numbers of troops were held back from the front. Because of those fears, plus actual depredations by Negroes and deserters, at times more than 50,000 men were scattered far back behind the front lines and throughout all the Confederate states. Governors retained militia contingents because of the clamor for protection, keeping more and more as the war went on. These totaled probably twice as many men as the number of behind-the-lines Confederate troops. The withholding of 150,000 to 200,000 men—at one time a third of the

Confederate fighting forces—away from the front, was a strain the South could not afford if it wished to wage a successful war. Of course the militiamen were often merely malingerers trying to avoid active service, men who did not wish to fight and might actually have obstructed the war effort had they been taken into battle. Even so, the Confederate states were occupied by their own soldiery long before being occupied by Northern troops. And one of the major reasons was precisely the fear of Negro uprisings.

Actually more than any Negro resistance—more apt to manifest itself in malingering or secret sabotage than in overt aggression—the breakdown of the slave system, ever more rapidly as the war went on, was a factor in undermining Southern resistance more dangerous than any Negro insurrection. This breakdown promoted the war within a war, gave it an impetus it might not have achieved had not sheer inexorable economics been at work.

In the first place, King Cotton was dethroned almost at the outset of the war, and that was the chief slave crop, the *raison d'être* of slavery. Cotton had to be warehoused or burned. Some was seized or bought by the Confederate or state governments but remuneration was slow in coming and was in ever more worthless currency and treasury notes. The profits now went not so much to the grower as to the speculators and blockade runners. As a result of curtailed production, the value of slaves went down with the price of cotton. The slaveowner saw a vast portion of his capital wiped out.

Negroes could be impressed just as other property, and the owner believed that the prices the government paid were only a fraction of what they should be. Often payment was long delayed or never made. All through the war, plantation owners fought against impressment without their consent, as well as for larger payments. Many owners found escape from impending bankruptcy only by farming their slaves out to the government to build roads, erect fortifications, or as cooks, camp attendants, muleteers. They insisted on receiving for them a wage nearly four times that of the enlisted white soldier. They were more apt to get paid than the soldier was to receive his stipend. When they did not, the owners withdrew their Negroes or refused to send them. There was practically a labor boycott of the Confederacy when at one time it wished to reduce such payments.

But as cotton-growing became less profitable, as the worth of slaves deteriorated, and as the cost of maintaining them increased, a powerful clamp closed on the necks of the largest owners.

The exodus from the plantations swelled to a mighty river of Negroes seeking food, seeking a new life, seeking freedom. From the very first, large numbers of Negroes began camping outside Federal lines. Some roamed freely through the camps picking up what morsels of food or discarded clothing they could find. At first, most of the Northern commanders repulsed them, and many permitted Southern slave-hunters to enter the camps to ferret out those who had run away, for which they were sometimes commended by Southern newspapers. One Negro commented ruefully that the road back to slavery was lighted by the gleam of Northern bayonets.

General Grant never permitted slave-hunters and gave refugees aid. General John C. Fremont, Union Commander of the Western Department, and General David Hunter, Commander of the Department of the South, with headquarters in South Carolina, both promptly declared all slaves freed, for which they were severely (and correctly) [1] reprimanded. Fremont was removed. Secretary of War Edwin Stanton hastened to reassure the South that no measures leading to slave insurrection would be taken—a blindness of the times, both social and military.

As battles began going badly for the South, and as cotton planting diminished, more owners simply kicked their slaves off their properties. One owner near Carrollton, Louisiana, drove them off to the Yankee lines. "The Yankees are king here now, so go to your king for food and shelter." As the exodus grew greater, black refugees lay in great heaps, hungry and sick, outside every Union picket line. "I cannot receive them," Gen-

---

[1] They had no authority to issue such an order.

eral Phelps wrote Washington, "for I have neither work, shelter nor the means . . . of transporting them to Haiti." Since it was intolerable to drive them back to slavery or to expose them to the inevitable brutalities of the enemy, he suggested that able blacks be enlisted and become an agent of order and a guard against the loss of their new liberty. Getting no satisfaction from his superior, General Butler, or from the War Department, he resigned and went back to his farm in Vermont.

Butler, though once an anti-Negro Democrat, was one of the first to take realistic action to handle the slave refugees. On the ramparts of Fort Monroe, the flag-officer, who commanded the ships employed in the attack, said, "General, . . . in less than twenty-four hours deserting slaves will commence swarming to your lines. They should be helped so they will not be used to work on enemy fortifications." This was as necessary as capturing and destroying enemy batteries. When the next slaves came in, Butler ordered them put to work as contraband of war. But he paid them ten dollars a month wages plus their rations. He also deducted enough to provide for destitute nonworkers, a method soon imitated by all Federal commanders and presently legalized by general military orders, later used by the Freedmen's Bureau to provide social welfare, schools, and medical care. One superintendent later put it, "Not one cent of money was ever drawn from the Government for their freedom on any account."

The escape of slaves from the plantations, whether voluntary or involuntary, into a state of quasi-freedom, however miserable, was part of the black insurrection, part of the breakdown of the slave and plantation system. The incorporation of such refugees into the Union armies became a militant phase of that changed status and in itself helped create a new spirit among all Negroes, leading more of them to leave and to revolt. This process of obtaining arms did not proceed rapidly until after the Emancipation Proclamation, though prior Congressional legislation allowed them to enlist both in the North and in the South. The attitude of Union commanders little by little changed to meet the new conditions. Special officers of high rank, such as Lorenzo Thomas, the Adjutant General, were sent to Federal army units in the South to implement and enforce the new regulations. They had the authority to reduce in rank or throw out officers who refused to follow the new regulations, and they used this authority to threaten dismissal to those of the various field staffs who did not actively promote the new policies.

Even so, some black enlistment occurred prior to the over-all regulations. Even before the Congressional law, some 10,000 Negroes in the Mississippi area were recruited and armed. Probably the first to act was Major-General David Hunter in South Carolina. One fine morning he appeared with twirling glasses, puckered lips and dilated nostrils, and ordered the formation of a black regiment to fight for freedom, which he declared was the issue of the war.

Kentucky Congressman C. A. Wycliffe raised hob with the War Department: by what right had he organized a regiment of fugitive slaves? Hunter's airy reply indicates the extent to which ideas of new freedom animated the Negroes. He denied that any fugitive slaves had been recruited,

> only a fine regiment of loyal persons whose late masters are fugitive rebels . . . who everywhere fly before the appearance of the national flag, leaving their loyal and unhappy servants behind them, to shift as best they can for themselves. . . . Far from trying to evade the presence of their late owners . . . they are now, one and all, endeavoring with commendable zeal to acquire the drill and discipline requisite . . . to go in full and effective pursuit of their fugacious and treacherous protectors.

The only Negroes he had found were anxious "to welcome us, and aid us and supply us with food, labor and information." Were he not otherwise engaged he could enlist not one but five or six such loyal regiments. By fall he hoped to have up to fifty thousand of "these hardy and devoted soldiers." [2]

---

[2] The fact that General Hunter proved himself repeatedly to be totally unfit to command troops, weakened this and later statements. Indeed it is interesting that Hunter, Butler and, above all, Fremont,

It was ironic that South Carolina, which had initiated the Ci⟨vil⟩ War, should be the first state to feel the impact of the bla⟨ck⟩ insurrection in the form of armed Negro troops. The regime⟨nt⟩ saw its initial fighting on Saint Helena Island, then raided throug⟨h⟩ Georgia and Florida. "They fought with astonishing coolne⟨ss⟩ and bravery," reported their commander, "and deserve all prais⟨e.⟩" General Rufus Saxon reported that within a month after bei⟨ng⟩ recruited, these "untrained soldiers have captured from the ene⟨my⟩ . . . property equal in value to the cost of the regiment fo⟨r a⟩ year, besides destroying salt-works along the coast." This ⟨was⟩ a serious loss for the South where the cost of salt had gon⟨e up⟩ 1,000 per cent and was often unobtainable.

The dangers for black troops were far greater than for ⟨white⟩ troops. Not only were they apt to be sent on the most dang⟨erous⟩ missions, but when taken prisoner they were likely to be ⟨tor⟩tured and cruelly murdered. The massacre of Negro pri⟨soners⟩ in the Fort Pillow engagement is one of the most awful ep⟨isodes⟩ in the whole history of war through all the ages.

As the struggle went on, it became ever more evident t⟨hat the⟩ South simply did not have enough manpower to fight a w⟨ar and⟩ at the same time fight Negroes and deserters and armed ⟨Union⟩ists behind the lines. By early 1864 Secretary of State J⟨udah⟩ Benjamin openly advocated emancipation in the hope t⟨hat it⟩ might bring sympathy for the South in Europe and perh⟨aps⟩ recognition. He was excoriated by most of the then v⟨arious⟩ ments of the South. By the end of the year President D⟨avis and⟩ General Lee were advocating the arming of Negro tro⟨ops who⟩ as part of their reward would be emancipated, as w⟨ould their⟩ families. Lee went even farther, declaring that a progr⟨am should⟩ be worked out for the gradual emancipation of *all* sl⟨aves⟩ unless this were done it would be done by the Nort⟨h.⟩

---

strongly in favor of immediate emancipation, were all m⟨ilitary⟩ asses, unfit to lead even a platoon, except to disaster. ⟨They⟩ were clutching at straws in urging measures designed ⟨to keep the⟩ eyes of their superiors away from their own blunders.

wry admission that the war had been a vast mistake. It wiped out the principal Southern cause and reason for the war.

The proposed bill calling for the enlistment of 200,000 slaves—with the consent of their masters—was bitterly opposed by the Confederate Congress and was finally voted down on February 8, 1865. As the black clouds gathered over the land, with the Federal armies closing in on all sides, it was finally enacted on March 9, but without any emancipation clause, and of course too late. The call for volunteers in Richmond brought exactly twenty Negroes to the colors. They were uniformed in gray and marched triumphantly through the city, receiving much applause, chiefly from the ladies. The response was no better anywhere else. Negroes were then made subject to the draft from April 2 on—too late, for on that day Davis abandoned Richmond.

The Negro revolt against the Confederacy, at first largely passive, all during the war moved on to more militant awareness and action, and even those who had not been drawn into the conflict expressed their joy over the new freedom, sometimes in extravagant and bizarre ways.

Union General Edward H. Ripley of the XXIV Corps, in his *Personal Recollections* told about the march into Richmond after Davis fled. "The air was darkened by the thick tempest of black smoke and cinders which swept the streets, and as we penetrated deeper into the city, the bands were temporarily drowned by the crashing of falling walls, the roar of flames, and the terrific explosion of shells in the burning warehouses." The entry was up Main Street to the Exchange Hotel, and the way was jammed with thousands of Negroes who until that moment had been slaves. They threw themselves down on their hands and knees almost under the horses' feet to pray and give thanks in the wild delirium of their sudden deliverance. Floods of tears poured down their faces, and they threw their hands into the air, shouting, "Glory to God! Glory to God! The day of jubilee hab come! Massa Linkum am here! Massa Linkum am here!"

On the march of Grant's army from Spottsylvania to the North Anna river, reported the New York *Tribune*, Negro families

were gathered along the roadside, grinning all over their faces. "Massa's gone away, Gemmen," was the universal comment. "He went away right smart last night, dat's all I knows." A nearly blind Negro, frosted with eighty-five winters, said chuckling, "I'se been waiting for you gemmen sometime. I know you was coming 'cause I heard Massa and Missus talking about you."

9. The Last Mile

The old mules, the ones not requisitioned for war, began dropping in the furrows. Old Negroes, too. More Negroes fled from the plantations, or simply went adrift because their owners could no longer afford to feed them or, in some cases, threw them out. Railroads began breaking down; old wagons and carriages went to pieces. The roads could not be repaired. Numbers of cities, even when food was available in adjacent rural areas, began to suffer from near starvation. More food riots broke out. People were unable to buy food, even if they had money, for banks began closing down; still others, for the same reason, received no wages. Often those who had a little money could not buy enough to eat because of inflation. After the fall of Vicksburg in July, 1863, not a chicken could get through the Mississippi River blockade and from then on large areas were doomed to inadequate food supplies. Early in the war, the value of money had started to slide. By the time of Appomattox, treasury notes were worth only 1.6 cents on the dollar. Prices of food and necessities became absolutely astronomical. A month's soldier's pay, on which hundreds of thousands were dependent, would buy only a fifth of a bag of flour. On her wild flight from Richmond with her children, Mrs. Davis had to pay a hundred Confederate dollars for crackers and a glass of milk. Half-starving soldiers at the front near Richmond sent part of their rations to Richmond where people were rioting for food.

Substitutes were utilized: sorghum because there was no sugar, parched sweet potatoes, corn, or rye instead of coffee. Though many small farmers ate as well as usual and speculators, traders, and hoarders could banquet, even the best tables in Richmond were reduced to serving cornbread and pea soup. Meat was often missing for a month at a time. A guest at Secretary Benjamin's house was served cornbread smeared with English walnut paste (from a tree in the yard), a dab of bacon, and wine. A bon vivant, he was never without wine.

Small children, whether Negro or white, were stunted in their growth, fell prey to the diseases of poverty or died. Soldiers were increasingly stricken with disease, and epidemics spread to the home front. There was little medicine other than dubious home-made remedies. Hospitals in Richmond itself often had no bandages for the wounded.

As candles and pine tapers replaced lamps, little reading could be done at night. Nor could complaints be easily penned, for there was no ink, only quick-fading stain from oak-balls and poke berries.

As the war went on, more of the press turned against Davis, even the Richmond papers, although of course the Richmond *Examiner*, the Charleston *Mercury*, the Raleigh *Standard*, most Arkansas papers, and most of the Whig papers, as in Natchez, were hostile in varying degrees throughout the war if not openly pro-Union. Following Gettysburg the chorus grew louder. The good humor of editors was not enhanced as both ink and paper became harder to get and more expensive. Some had to resort to printing on wrapping paper or waste paper—in short, anything available. For a time even the official paper of Jackson, Mississippi, had to be printed on wallpaper.

The picture was not evenly drawn. In some regions the people had almost a superabundance of food and other scarce goods, because of local conditions, isolation, or lack of means to ship things out. Even with all the hardships, the South up to the very end still had great resources and manpower. Men and revolutionists, nations and countries, have fought on with unbreakable courage in the face of worse disasters and with far inferior means and weapons. Davis was the last important bitter-ender to know this and was willing to stake his life on it.

But the will to fight had ebbed; the insurrection behind the lines had spread far and wide, and the peace parties and allied secret societies had penetrated every corner of the Confederacy. From the beginning the South had had to fight a war before the lines and behind the lines.

After Lee's final attempt to invade the North failed at Gettysburg, he foresaw the dreadful ordeals ahead; his health almost broke, and he tried to resign. Unable to accomplish what he himself desired, how—he wrote Davis—could he fulfill the expectations of others? Davis wrote back that he could find no one else to take his place. Without Lee the war would almost certainly have collapsed at once, and a year of futile bloodshed would have been avoided.

As internal disaffection increased and the probability of defeat became more apparent, the Richmond regime, in the manner customary to all crumbling systems, resorted to increased violations of human rights, tighter laws against conspiracy and subversion, the abolition of yet more civil liberties and more brutal use of the police and military forces. It merely made opposition more widespread, bitter, and determined, creating more resistance than it abolished. It cost a thousand dollars a head to round up a deserter, and this soon mounted into millions. But even if captured, he was only a liability. Deserters could rarely be induced to fight, shirked all their duties and deserted again at the first opportunity, or else returned home or joined an armed band of outlaws. They could no longer be shot, though many were, particularly in the beginning, for this would have caused mass uprisings. Before they could be court-martialed, a judge would issue a writ of *habeas corpus*, and so strong was the feeling about this sacred instrument that the army usually had to honor it. They could scarcely be tried in a civil court, for rarely could a jury be found to convict evaders. And if they were put in jail, often armed men released them.

Resistance increasingly also took on a legal guise, as laws were passed modifying or restricting the high-handed activities of the military, of impressment and of the draft agents; tax collections were made more difficult; legal rights were established for militia-men; and the numbers of those eligible for draft exemption was increased. South Carolina, most responsible for the bloody fiasco, now assumed much the same position it had thirty-five years earlier with its Nullification Acts (which had necessitated the sending in of Federal troops) but this time against the laws of the Confederacy. It nullified the Confederate laws of impressment of goods and services.

Thus the Federal victories, the retreat to Appomattox, and Sherman's long devastating march that cut off food and supplies, were aided by the prolonged war within a war, which broke out in new unanticipated quarters and began to directly involve important leaders. The writing on the wall was now visible to nearly everybody. Large numbers of people appeared at all Federal outposts, especially in Georgia, to swear fealty to the Union, to ask for protection, to be given assurances about their homes and their rights to take produce to market. Sherman told them to organize and issued identification cards, which his men would recognize, and he offered them armed protection if necessary.

Confederate control progressively broke down over vast areas. The number of plundering marauders increased. These had no principles and no loyalties; they were merely desperate, hungry men. In certain parts, more destruction was wrought and looting was done by such outlaws than by the invading armies, especially when Sherman went through, for however implacable his scorched-earth policy, he held, in the main, to strategic objectives.

Well before the fall of Richmond, President Davis was having sleepless nights. His spirit was never broken, but it was badly corroded by bitter attacks, the fear and treachery of those about him, and the harsh onslaughts in much of the press. Loud-mouthed railers almost disrupted the Confederacy before the end came. Mrs. Davis was frequently in tears over the ugly attacks and innuendos, often by erstwhile friends and original firebrands, men who had once aroused the populace in support of secession and now aroused it against Davis and his government. She came to hate Rhett of South Carolina more than Lincoln. Many die-hard advocates of slavery, annoyed by wartime burdens, taxes, and blunders, became more virulent than pro-Unionists, peace advocates, or abolitionists.

The day came when cannon rattled the windows in the capital city. In church, women rose from their pews screaming and rushed out to look after their children and sick ones. Davis, wasted and gaunt, put his arms about his wife Varina, and told her she must take her young sister Maggie and the children south to safety. He gave her money and a small pistol, showing her how to use it. He planned to set up a new capital somewhere in the state, although just where he had not decided.

Her experiences tell us a great deal about the breakdown of the South, the hardships, the widespread desire for peace, the changed attitude of the people. The engine of the dilapidated train she took broke down just outside the city, and she and her brood, baby Winnie in her arms, had to sit there all night, listening to the cries and moans of fear, the booming of artillery, the running feet of distraught workmen.

They finally reached Danville on the southern edge of the state. Friends wanted her to rest there, but she kept on, this time in a crowded sleeping car. The rain was pouring down, the car roof leaked, their beds and baggage were soaked, a deluge that kept up all the way to Charlotte, North Carolina, and which was to continue all through April and on in to May as she moved on through Georgia.

The people were now aware that collapse was at hand, the prognostications of the men of the war within a war were coming to pass, and they feared reprisals if they helped Varina. Not a door in the city opened to provide her a place to sleep. She encountered no friends, only despair, terror, cold-eyed hate, until finally an old Jew rented her a house. He was so kind, he remained an enduring blessed memory in her heart all the rest of her life.

On April 2, Lee telegraphed Davis that he was evacuating Petersburg, that the President must get out of Richmond that same night. The President packed only groceries and took some bedding, but sent the family carriage to the station to be put on a flatcar. It was held for a later train and he never saw it again. Two days later from Danville he issued a weird proclamation, describing the evacuation of Richmond as merely military strategy to give the Confederate forces freedom of action so they could strike out in any direction. Triumph was certain; all that was needed was unconquerable determination. He soon had to flee on to Greensboro, North Carolina.

The people there were not happy about the arrival of Davis, his cabinet and his large entourage. All doors remained closed. A staff member finally found a small room and shared it with him. Another under-officer found Secretary of State Benjamin wandering about in the driving rain unable to find any place to stay and did the same. The rest of the cabinet and staff was obliged to remain in the leaky railway coaches. A Negro boy prepared what little food was available on an outside fire under a shed. Each day Davis, half-sick, badly wasted away, struggled through deep mud to the dripping cars to transact state business.

General Johnston told him he had to surrender. His artillery could scarcely be moved, for deserters, leaving in droves, had run off with the mule teams. General Beauregard also insisted that further resistance was impossible. Lee had already surrendered at Appomattox. Davis had to authorize negotiations and went on to Charlotte to catch up with Varina.

She had already gone on. No one would receive him, and he finally found lodging in the quarters of a convivial Northern bachelor, the local express agent. Wade Hampton, the greatest slaveowner in America, wrote him from Hillsboro that they could never live under a base and vulgar Northern tyranny. If they fought on, they could still look forward to European intervention. If he had 20,000 men he could whip Sherman within twenty days. He suggested that what infantry was left be converted into cavalry, and that they keep up the fight in Texas. If the worst came to the worst they would go to Mexico. This Davis was already planning to do.

But Benjamin said that even if they could raise 10,000 men,

there was no way to arm them. All supplies of powder and lead had been cut off. Texas was cut off by Yankee gunboats. He urged Davis to proclaim the facts to the people, ratify the surrender agreement with Sherman, and resign. He himself was going to escape to England via the West Indies, which he did a few days later disguised as a farmer in homespun. All his cabinet was of the same mind. Davis should resign. Nine-tenths of the people, Navy Secretary Mallory wrote him, were weary of war and wanted peace. Davis was not willing to surrender without getting terms, but Johnston signed an unconditional surrender without even consulting him and, angry and embittered, he hurried on to catch up with Varina, see her to safety and then go on to Texas.

It was now dangerous to keep on with such a large entourage. On reaching South Carolina, he dismissed those of his cabinet still with him, except for Postmaster Reagan who insisted on staying by his side, and dispersed all his cavalry force except ten picked men, handing over what little of the treasury remained in his hands. Their morale was gone; he knew they would not fight.

"I saw an organized government disintegrate and fall in pieces . . ." wrote his confidential clerk, "until there was left only a single member of his cabinet, his private secretary, a few members of his staff, a few guides and servants to represent what had once been a powerful government."

The flight of Varina and Jefferson Davis is an epic of misery that reveals the final breakdown and chaos in South Carolina and Georgia, the terror of armed hungry bands, the spread of disease, the smallpox epidemic, the hordes of returning soldiers, some barefoot and ragged, sick, maimed, blind, the lack of food. Varina walked through endless miles of deep mud, her baby in her arms, had her inoculated against smallpox by the scab of a Negro boy. There were the nights on the cold ground, weeping the whole night through, and their final capture shortly after Davis caught up with her.

The war was over, the war within a war would soon be over.

The anti-Confederate resistance fighters were too heterogeneous, too dispersed, too varied in their aims and hopes to reap the benefits of their long heroic struggle. They were unable to project their movement on into the postwar period. Most of them were caught in the web of economic and social collapse, forced, along with everybody else, into a desperate struggle for personal survival, which required a new kind of heroism.

A few resistance leaders were utilized by the occupation. Holden, Brownlow, and William L. Sharkey became governors. Brown of Georgia, as did many others, quickly allied himself with Reconstruction and the carpetbaggers, supported the most radical new measures and thereby added millions to his already large fortune. When passions finally cooled, he was able to return to politics and serve in the United States Senate.

Those who had merely wanted peace, now had peace, but it was the peace of unconditional surrender. Those who believed in the preservation of the Union were now back in the Union, but not entirely; a long twilight of years of nonparticipation in the national life was to come. The chasm between the rich and the poor, always so great in a feudal society, had grown wider and deeper during the war, but the resistance of the have-nots brought them few economic benefits, and for the most part their lot was worse. The small farmers who had long resisted the slavocracy were often reduced to the status of sharecroppers and tenants. The more lawless elements who had learned to live by plunder and violence, and were now forced to gain a living in more orderly ways, were scarcely content with the new system. The Negroes briefly gained a few political and economic rights, soon to be lost. But their new freedom permitted them to enjoy a degree of education not previously available. Limited possibilities for personal advancement were opened up. Liberty of movement provided the chance to escape from the most intolerable situations.

Before the end of the war, the peace movement had penetrated to every corner of the Confederacy and operated both secretly and openly. But the particular areas of more militant armed resistance throw light on the economic and political sources of revolt, of which often the participants were only vaguely aware. Its strongest manifestations were in the nonslave areas of the mountains and hill regions. These stretched solidly from east Tennessee and West Virginia deep into Georgia and Alabama. Northwestern Mississippi and northwestern Arkansas were also mountainous and similarly peopled by independent farmers. Among these people lay the core of resistance to the war. Guerrilla bands operated in central Texas and in the rough mountains along the Rio Grande. Winn Parish, typical of the red-clay scrub pine country from Louisiana to the Carolinas, refused to secede. It produced little cotton, had few slaves and actually depended on lumbering. Such counties were cool toward secession and in many, if not all, armed bands were active.

All the high backland country harbored small independent proprietors, who cherished their isolation and were among the most independent people the world has known. They had been at odds with slaveholders and large plantation owners long before the Civil War, a running battle that went back several centuries (Bacon's rebellion in Virginia had occurred in 1675). They had often fought for freeholder rights, for proper representation, and for more equitable taxation, as well as for their share of state improvements and public works. Well before the Civil War their feuds with the cotton areas had often flamed into armed revolt. It is perhaps significant that much of this area belongs to the Appalachian region, now dubbed as a poverty area to be aided (or so it is presumed) by Federal undertakings. Is it a belated recognition of evils that have prevailed there for centuries?

Other pockets of resistance existed along the Gulf Coast in northern and central Florida, all swamp country, in the Mississippi and Alabama bayou country, and, increasingly, along the Atlantic coast, where people were accustomed to live by other crops than cotton and to depend on outside trade.

The war within a war was a disjointed, almost inchoate movement, though, as time went on, in northern mountains areas of discontent and the discontented were welded and worked together. But there was more class consciousness among the slave-holders than among their foes. An officer, bringing Aughey word of his impending trial and execution, asked him peevishly why an educated person had not cast his lot in with the ruling aristocracy. But as time went on the slogan, "rich man's war, poor man's fight," gained more currency. So far as its spokesmen were articulate, its stated aims were rarely expressed in economic terms. Its spiritual food came from the Declaration of Independence, the Bill of Rights and the thinking of Thomas Jefferson. It advocated and fought for the inviolacy of civil and human rights even in wartime, a belief in states' rights not to uphold slavery but to preserve human liberties, an enduring loyalty to the Union as a whole and, above all, a deep desire for peace and the solution of problems by reason, not force. These were all basic American doctrines. Most resistors were motivated also by economic considerations, often selfishly so, but still were largely unconscious of the deeper social forces. In any event, the movement was promoted and it grew because of brave individuals, men willing to risk everything for what they held dear and believed right.

After the war, though some Northern elements were aware of the problems, and in a sense President Andrew Johnson himself was their spokesman—which perhaps is one basic reason for the attempt to impeach him—the Radical Republicans advocated harsh punitive measures and became aligned with the new eager corporate interests taking over Southern resources and properties. They soon allied themselves, not with the yeomanry of the South but with the long-standing privileged groups, the old group of plantation owners who thereby saved much of both their wealth and their position.

With peace, militancy declined and the old bonds of rebellion were weakened or destroyed. The new militants were those of the counterrevolution, the old-time vigilantes inaugurating a new reign of terror against both the Negro and white freedom-loving elements. General Nathaniel Bedford Forrest, a slave-trader before the war, headed the Ku Klux Klan in his state.

The mystique of the South, its sectional patriotism, which had sent so many off to the front who had nothing whatever to gain from the war, reasserted itself strongly, precisely because of prolonged military occupation, plus the difficulties of making a living, and the fears, often artificially created, of racial equality. The Negro was a competitor in a new way, a competitor for jobs, land, and freedom. These feelings made worse by the web of ruin, dislocation, and misery. In due time the counterrevolution, if it may be called that, won the day; the Negro was stripped of his voting rights and other freedoms, condemned to Jim Crowism, limited in his job and educational opportunities, and finally forced to accept planned inferiority.

We are still too close to the Civil War, still too uninformed, to appreciate all of its social and cultural manifestations and results or to comprehend the intricate emotions and desires that then and since have moved the hearts and minds of men both North and South. Even the wisest among us know little about such things. But the principles for which many Southern men of the war within a war fought with such courage and loyalty are part of our abiding heritage. The old proslavery leaders, the die-hards of a lost cause, have been glamourized in fact and fiction, even in the North. But the real Southern heroes, those of the war within a war, have had no hearing, have in fact gone unsung and unhonored into the twilight of history. If this work has had a purpose, it is to preserve the memory of their deeds.

Selected Bibliography

ALFRIEND, FRANK H. *Life of Jefferson Davis.* Cincinnati and Philadelphia, 1868.

ANDREWS, ELIZA F. *War-Time Journal of a Georgia Girl, 1864–5.* New York, 1908.

ANDREWS, E. W. and C. M. (eds.). *Journal of a Lady of Quality.* New Haven, 1921.

ANDREWS, GARNETT. *Reminiscences of an Old Georgia Lawyer.* Atlanta, 1870.

APTHEKER, HERBERT. *A Documentary History of the Negro People in the United States.* New York, 1951.

ARNOLD, ISAAC N. *History of Abraham Lincoln and the Overthrow of Slavery.* Chicago, 1866.

ASCHE, S. A. *History of North Carolina.* 2 vols. Raleigh, 1925.

AUGHEY, JOHN H. *Tupelo.* Lincoln, Nebraska, 1888.

AVERY, I. W. *The History of the State of Georgia from 1850 to 1881.* New York, 1881.

BAKER, RAY STANDARD. *Following the Color Line.* New York, 1964 (paperback reprint).

BANCROFT, FREDERIC. *Slave Trading in the Old South.* Baltimore, 1931.

BASSETT, J. S. *Anti-Slavery Leaders of North Carolina.* Baltimore, 1898.

BEERS, FANNIE A. *Memories . . . or Four Years of War.* Philadelphia, 1888.

BENTON, THOMAS HART. *Thirty Years View . . . 1820–1850.* 2 vols. New York, 1857.

BETTERSWORTH, JOHN K. *Confederate Mississippi.* Baton Rouge, 1943.

BISHOP, A. W. *Loyalty on the Frontier, or Sketches of Union Men of the Southwest.* St. Louis, 1863.

BLAINE, JAMES G. *Twenty Years of Congress.* Norwich, 1884.

BONDURANT, ALEXANDER. "Did Jones County Secede?" *Mississippi Historical Society.* I, 104–106, 1898.

BROWN, WILLIAM WELLS. *The Negro in the American Rebellion.* Boston, 1880.

BROWNLOW, W. G. *Sketches of the Rise, Progress and Decline of Secession . . . Personal Adventures among the Rebels.* Philadelphia, 1862.

BUTLER, PIERCE. *Judah P. Benjamin.* Philadelphia, 1906.

CALLAHAN, J. M. *Semi-Centennial History of West Virginia.* Charleston, 1913.

CAMPBELL, J. A. *Jefferson Davis . . . A Memoir by His Wife.* 2 vols. New York, 1890.

——. *Recollection of the Evacuation of Richmond.* Baltimore, 1880.

CAPERS, HENRY D. *The Life and Times of C. J. Memminger.* Richmond, 1893.

CHESTNUT, MARY BOYKIN. *Diary from Dixie.* New York, 1905.

CHRISTIAN, E. ASHBURY. *Richmond, Her Past and Present.* Richmond, 1912.

CLAY, CLEMENT C. *A Belle of the Fifties.* New York, 1904.

CLELAND, ROBERT G. "Jefferson Davis and the Confederate Congress," *Southwest Historical Quarterly.* XIX, 215–231.

CLEVELAND, HENRY. *Alexander H. Stephens.* Philadelphia, 1866.

"Conduct of Negroes During the War, Extracts from the Diary of Edmund Ruffin," *William and Mary College Quarterly.* XXII, No. 4, 258–262.

DAVIS, JEFFERSON. *Rise and Fall of the Confederate Government.* 2 vols. New York, 1881.

DAVIS, WASHINGTON. *Camp Fire Chats of the Civil War.* Chicago, 1884.

DAVIS, WILLIAM W. *Civil War and Reconstruction in Florida.* New York, 1913.

DE BOW, J. D. B. (ed.). *The Industrial Resources of the Confederate Government.* 2 vols. New York, 1881.

DE LEON, T. C. *Four Years in Rebel Capitals.* Atlanta, 1890.

DENMAN, CLARENCE P. *The Secession Movement in Alabama.* Montgomery, 1933.

DODD, W. E. *Jefferson Davis.* Philadelphia, 1907.

DOWD, CLEMENT. *Life of Zebulon B. Vance.* Charlotte, 1897.

DUBOSE, JOHN WITHERSPOON. *The Life and Times of William Lounwes Yancey.* Birmingham, 1892.

DYER, JOHN WILL. *Reminiscences; or Four Years in the Confederate Army.* Evansville, 1898.

ECHENRODE, H. J. *Jefferson Davis.* New York, 1923.

EDMONDS, GEORGE. *Facts and Falsehoods Concerning the War on the South, 1861–65.* Memphis, 1904.

EGGLESTON, GEORGE C. *A Rebel's Recollections.* New York, 1887.

ELLIS, DANIEL. *Thrilling Adventures of Daniel Ellis, the Great American Guide of East Tennessee.* New York, 1867.

FLEMING, WALTER L. *Jefferson Davis, The Negroes and the Negro Problem.* Baton Rouge, 1908.

——. "The Peace Movement in Alabama During the Civil War," *South Atlantic Quarterly.* II, April–July, 1903, pp. 114–24, 246–60.

FOOTE, HENRY S. *A Cachet of Reminiscences.* Washington, 1874.

——. *War of Rebellion, or Scylla and Charybdis.* New York, 1866.

FREEMAN, DOUGLAS SOUTHALL. *Robert E. Lee, A Biography.* 4 vols. New York, 1934, 1935, 1936.

GILMORE, JAMES R. *Among the Pines or Southern Secession Time.* New York, 1862.

GIPSOM, LAWRENCE H. "The Collapse of the Confederacy," *Mississippi Historical Review.* XI, 54–55, 1918.

GORDON, JOHN B. *Reminiscences of the Civil War.* New York, 1903.

GRANT, ULYSSES S. *Personal Memoirs.* 2 vols. New York, 1885–6.

GREELEY, HORACE. *The American Conflict.* Hartford, Chicago, 1864–66.

HAMILTON, J. G. DE ROULHAC. "Heroes of America," *Southern Historical Association,* January, 1907, pp. 10–19.

HAY, THOMAS R. "Davis-Hood-Johnston Controversy in 1864," *Mississippi Historical Review.* XI, 54–55.

——. "The South and the Arming of the Slaves," *Mississippi Historical Review.* VI.

HENRY, C. S. "Negro Sentiment in the Civil War," *North American Review.* Vol. 95.

HESSELTINE, WILLIAM B. *The Tragic Conflict.* New York, 1962.

HILL, BENJAMIN H., Jr. *Senator Benjamin Hill of Georgia . . . Speeches and Writings.* Atlanta, 1891.

HILL, D. H. *Bethel to Sharpsburg: North Carolina in the War Between the States.* 2 vols. Raleigh, 1926.

HILL, LOUISE BILES. *Joseph E. Brown and the Confederacy.* Chapel Hill, 1939.

HODGSON, JOSEPH. *The Cradle of the Confederacy: or the Times of Troup, Quitman and Yancey.* Mobile, 1876.

HOLDEN, W. W. *Memoirs*. Durham, North Carolina, 1911.

HOPLEY, CATHERINE C. *Life in the South; from the Commencement of the War*. London, 1863.

HOYT, W. H. *The Mecklenberg Declaration of Independence*. New York, 1907.

HUMES, THOMAS W. *The Loyal Mountaineer of Tennessee*. Knoxville, 1888.

HUSE, CALEB. *The Supplies for the Confederacy*. Boston, 1904.

JOHNSON, CHARLES BENEULYN. *Muskets and Medicine*. Philadelphia, 1917.

JOHNSON, R. V., and BUEL, C. C. *Battles and Leaders of the Civil War*. 4 vols. New York, 1887.

JOHNSTON, JOSE E. *Narrative of Military Operations during the War between the States*. New York, 1874.

JOHNSTON, RICHARD M. and BROWNE, WM. H. *Life of Alexander H. Stephens*. Philadelphia, 1878.

JONES, JOHN B. *A Rebel War Clerk's Diary at the Confederate States' Capital*. 2 vols. Philadelphia, 1866.

JONES, JOHN W. *The Morale of the Confederate Army*. Atlanta, 1899.

KIMBALL, W. H. "Negro Soldiers in the Civil War," *Universalist Quarterly*. Vol. 33.

LE BREE, BENJAMIN. *The Confederate Soldier in the Civil War, 1861–65*. Louisville, 1895.

LEFFER, HUGH TALMAGE (ed.). *North Carolina History Told by Contemporaries*. Chapel Hill, 1934.

LOGAN, JOHN A. *The Great Conspiracy*. New York, 1866.

LONN, ELLA. *Desertion During the Civil War*. New York, 1928.

McGREGORY, JAMES CLYDE. *The Description of Virginia*. New York, 1922.

McNEILY, J. S. "War and Reconstruction in Mississippi, 1863–1890," *Mississippi Historical Society*. Vol. 2, 165–535, 1918.

MEADE, ROBERT D. "The Military Spirit of the South," *American Historical Review*. XXX, 55–60.

MARTIN, BESSIE. *Desertion of Alabama Troops from the Confederate Army*. New York, 1932.

MONTGOMERY, GOODE. "Alleged Secession of Jones County," *Mississippi Historical Review*. VIII, 13–22, 1904.

MOORE, ALBERT B. *Conscription and Conflict in the Confederacy*. New York, 1924.

MOORE, ALBERT B. *History of Alabama and Her People.* Chicago, 1927.

MOORE, FRANK. *The Rebellion Record.* 11 vols. New York, 1861–68.

MOORE, J. H. *Defense of the Mecklenberg Declaration of Independence.* Raleigh, 1908.

OLMSTED, FREDERICK LAW. *Journey in the Seaboard Slave States.* 2 vols. New York, 1856.

———. *Journeys and Explorations in the Cotton Kingdom.* 2 vols. London and New York, 1861.

OWSLEY, FRANK L. "Defeatism in the Confederacy," *North Carolina Historical Review.* III, 446–56, July, 1926.

———. "Local Defense and the Overthrow of the Confederacy," *Mississippi Valley Historical Review.* XI, 490–525, March, 1925.

———. *State Rights in the Confederacy.* Chicago, 1925.

PATTON, JAMES W. *Unionism and Reconstruction in Tennessee, 1860–69.* Chapel Hill, 1934.

PEARCE, HAYWOOD, JR. *Benjamin J. Hill.* Chicago, 1928.

PEPPER, GEORGE W. *Personal Recollections of Sherman's Campaigns in Georgia and the Carolinas.* Zanesville, Ohio, 1866.

PHILLIPS, ULRICH N. *Life of Robert Toombs.* New York, 1913.

POE, ORLANDO M. *Personal Recollections of the Occupation of East Tennessee and the Defense of Knoxville.* Detroit, 1889.

POLLARD, EDWARD A. *The Life of Jefferson Davis . . . Secret History of the Confederacy.* Philadelphia, 1869.

RAGAN, R. A. *Escape from East Tennessee.* Washington, 1910.

RAMSDELL, CHARLES W. *The Frontier and Secession.* New York, 1914.

ROSE, ARNOLD. *The Negro in America.* New York, 1964 (new ed., paperback).

ROWLAND, DUNBAR. *Jefferson Davis, Constitutionalist, His Letters, Papers and Speeches.* Jackson, Mississippi, 1923.

ROWLAND, ERON (Mrs. Dunbar R.). *Varina Howell, Wife of Jefferson Davis.* New York, 1927.

RUFFIN, EDMUND. *Agricultural, Geological and Descriptive Sketches of Lower North Carolina.* Raleigh, 1861.

RUSSELL, WILLIAM H. *The Civil War in America.* Richmond, 1861.

———. *My Diary, North and South.* 2 vols. London, 1863.

SCHURZ, CARL. *Reminiscences.* 3 vols. New York, 1907–8.

SHANKS, HENRY T. *The Secession Movement in Virginia, 1847–61.* Richmond, 1934.

SHERMAN, W. T. *Memoirs.* 2 vols. New York, 1886.

SPENCER, CORNELIA PHILLIPS. *The Last Ninety Days of the War in North Carolina.* New York, 1868.

STEPHENS, ALEXANDER H. *A Constitutional View of the Late War Between the States.* Philadelphia, 1868.

STEPHENSON, N. W. "The Question of Arming the Slaves," *American Historical Review.* XVIII, 205–308, January, 1919.

STOVALL, PLEASANT A. *Robert Toombs.* New York, 1892.

TATUM, GEORGIA L. *Disloyalty in the Confederacy.* Chapel Hill, 1934.

TEMPLE, OLIVER P. *East Tennessee and the Civil War.* Cincinnati, 1899.

THARIN, R. S. *Arbitrary Arrests in the Southern States from the Experience of an Alabama Unionist.* New York, 1863.

THOMAS, DAVID Y. *Arkansas in War and Reconstruction, 1861–74.* Little Rock, 1926.

TONEY, M. B. *Privations of a Private.* Nashville, 1905.

War of the Rebellion: A Compilation of the Official Records of the Union and Confederate Armies. 130 vols. Washington, 1880–1901.

WELLES, EDGAR T. *Diary.* 3 vols. Boston, 1911.

WEST, JOHN C. *Texan in Search of a Fight.* Waco, Texas, 1907.

WOODS, THOMAS H. "A Sketch of the Mississippi Secession Convention, 1861," *Mississippi Historical Review.* VI, 91–104, 1902.

WHITE, LAURA A. *Robert Barnwell Rhett.* New York, 1931.

WILLIAMS, S. C. *History of the Lost State of the Frontier.* Johnson City, Tennessee, 1924.

WILSON, JOSEPH T. *History of the Black Phalanx.*

WRIGHT, EDWARD. *Conscientious Objectors in the Civil War.* Philadelphia, 1931.

Index

: *171* :

Free Soil, 23, 24
Fremont, General John C., 144, 146
French, General W. H., 63
Fugitive Slave Law, 124

Gainesville, Fla., 71
Galveston, Texas, 3, 16, 26, 73
Ganut, General E. W., 25
Gardner, General F. K., 70
Georgia, 3, 4, 12–14, 19, 21, 64, 67, 68, 75, 114, 122–137, 147, 154, 155, 157, 159
Germans, 5, 26, 30
Gettysburg, 59, 152, 153
Gholson, General Samuel J., 112
Granger, General Gordon, 26, 27
Grant, General U. S., 19, 71, 72, 81, 115, 131, 144, 148
Great Smoky Mountains, 86
Greeley, Horace, 44, 134
Greene County, Miss., 118
Greensboro, N.C., 156
Greenville, Tenn., 81
Greenville County, S.C., 65
Guildford County, N.C., 21

Habeas corpus, 17, 21, 63, 73, 110, 113, 132–134, 137, 153
Hall, Leonard, 35
Ham, C. A., 88, 98
Hampshire County, W. Va., 41
Hampton Roads, Va., 136
Hampton, Wade, 156
Hancock County, Miss., 119
Harper's Ferry, W. Va., 142
Harris, Isham G., 78–81
Harrison County, Ala., 61

Heroes of America, 54–56, 62, 64, 66
Hill, Benjamin H., 122, 123, 135
Hill, Bergman H., 133
Hill, General D. H., 21, 64
Hill, Joshua, 19
Hill, Louise Bates, 122, 128
Hillsboro, N.C., 156
Hinds County, Miss., 95
Hobby, Colonel, 73
Holden, W. W., 3, 13, 14, 17, 20–22, 62, 158
Holston River Valley, Tenn., 75
Hood, General John B., 62, 128
Houston, Sam, 12, 25
Hunter, General David, 144
Hunter, Robert Taliaferro, 14
Huntsville, Ala., 60, 61

Impressment, 113, 116, 143, 153, 154
Impressment Act, 71
Impressment Laws, 13, 14, 18, 25, 129, 130
Indemnification, 23
Inflation, 15, 16
Irish, 5, 26, 30, 118
Iron Mountains, 75
Itawaba County, Miss., 117

Jackson, Miss., 93, 95, 96, 114, 115, 152
Jackson, Claiborn F., 24
Jackson County, Ala., 53
James Island, S.C., 1
James River, Va., 30
"Janissaries," 132
Jason County, Miss., 118
Jasper, Ala., 19

: *173* :

Vigilantes, 8, 9, 35, 54, 55, 79, 88, 93, 96, 100, 107, 114, 115, 140, 160

Virginia, 4, 5, 14, 29–47, 55, 57, 59, 61, 66, 75, 100, 103, 121, 126, 142, 159

Walter, H. W., 72

War Department, 13, 145, 146

War Department, Confederate, 113, 132

War of the Rebellion, 64

War Records, 97

Wartrace, Tenn., 90

Washington County, Miss., 110, 140

Washington, D.C., 5, 23, 31, 83, 144

Washington, George, 39

Watts, T. H., 23

Weitzel, General, 139

West Virginia, 29–47, 159

Wetzel County, W. Va., 35

Wheat, Jasper S., 35

Wheeling, W. Va., 29, 32, 33, 34, 35, 36, 38, 40, 41, 42

Whig, 3, 21, 22, 77, 80, 93, 96, 114, 121, 152

White, Rev. Martin, 23

White supremacy, 6, 7

Wigfall, Senator, 79, 84

Wilcox, General Cadmus, 65

Willey, William T., 36, 38, 42, 44

Williams, Joel, 117

Williams, Roger, 122

Winn Parish, La., 159

Winston County, Ala., 22

Wood, Colonel W. B., 85, 86

Woods, Samuel, 35

Wycliffe, C. A., 146

Yancey, William, 22, 53, 77, 84, 85

Yarborough, Professor Lorimer Vickeroy, 100, 102

Yarborough, Oscar, 101

Yeger, William, 115

Zapata County, Texas, 26

Zollicoffer, General F. K., 59, 84, 87

CARLETON BEALS is a veteran writer with thirty-eight books to his credit. Among his most recent books are *Nomads and Empire Builders: Native Peoples and Cultures of South America, Cyclone Carry: The Story of Carry Nation,* and *Eagles of the Andes,* all published by Chilton. The author lives and works in Killingworth, Connecticut.